For Maurice Rutherford

I wish to express my thanks to Angela Topping with whom I discussed some of the ideas contained in this book, to John Farrell for reading the first draft, but above all to Professor John Lucas who made the writing of the book possible and whose constructive and generous criticism put me right on certain points.

NOTHING EXTENUATE

A consideration of
Shakespeare's *Othello*

Matt Simpson

GREENWICH EXCHANGE
LONDON

Greenwich Exchange, London

First published in Great Britain in 2003

Nothing Extenuate – A consideration of Shakespeare's Othello
© Matt Simpson 2003

Printed and bound by Q3 Digital/Litho, Loughborough
Tel: 01509 213456
Typesetting and layout by Albion Associates, London
Tel: 020 8852 4646
Cover design by December Publications, Belfast
Tel: 028 90352059

Cover: Portrait of Moorish Ambassador to Queen Elizabeth I. Original owned by The Shakespeare Institute, University of Birmingham.

Greenwich Exchange Website: www.greenex.co.uk

ISBN 1-871551-71-4

Rightly to be great
Is not to stir without great argument.
But greatly to find quarrel in a straw,
When honour's at the stake.

Hamlet

Love is my religion – I could die for that.

Keats

Nuptial love maketh mankind; friendly love perfecteth it;
but wanton love corrupteth and embaseth it.

Bacon

CONTENTS

Preface – Every Minute is Expectancy

The only stage acting I have ever done was in a college production, in which I took the part of Iago. It was an exhilarating and somewhat frightening experience, in that I realised Iago is not a character you have to get studiously under the skin of but rather one who is already there, lurking beneath appearance, beneath our normal sincerities and whatever decency or honesty we may lay claim to, the potential or suppressed perversity in our make-ups – in a word, the potential psychopath. The frightening thing was the pleasure: I enjoyed being Iago almost to the point where I felt the tragedy was his. And though there is a case to be made for this – given our modern psychological knowledge and attitudes – it is, as I hope to show, ultimately a perverse view. Iago is the opposing voice, the spirit that denies, a man in league with Hell. In the less exalted words of the critic, John Wain: "Anybody who has been in the army, or worked in a factory, or even just knocked about with his eyes open, has met Iago." Wain calls him "a sharper with a dirty mind". He is our sarcasms over the breakfast table, the taint in our natures.

The exhilaration, of course, comes from the vicarious pleasure of being consistently wicked under a cloak of honesty. Part of the audience's pleasure comes from hearing Iago protest innocence and well-meaning effectively throughout the play: nobody on stage suspects him until it is too late; only the audience knows where he is heading. And this, of course, is the essential dramatic experience: it is like watching a particularly intense game of poker, with all its risk-taking, high-stakes artistry.

This exhilaration – with the play as a whole – has been sustained over many years of discussions with students. I am grateful for this opportunity to convey some of it in print.

1 We Must Obey the Time

Shakespeare is another country. The people speak a language at once familiar and unfamiliar, mostly organised as poetry. They have different customs, different expectations, different ways of accepting or worrying about the world they inhabit. To get the best out of a play like *Othello*, we have to make an effort of adjustment, to tune into this language and to understand underlying ideas once taken for granted that now either no longer obtain or have become open to question or blurred. At risk of sounding as though a simple formula to 'explain' is being offered, my account will, for example, rely on some knowledge of the doctrine of the humours to show that the *sanguine* humour is important to the play; it will also rely on knowledge of what was generally held to be the position of Man in an inevitably Christian hierarchically-arranged order of things – something the play accepts and at the same time seems to question. There is also a need to understand how culturally conditioned we are when it comes to symbolic values attached to colours – in this context most obviously black and white; also to register how vitally important are honour, reputation, good name when seen, particularly, as part of a soldier's way of life, and how manly honour is connected with and affected by honour in a civil context and in particular by sexual honour. We have to concede a reverence for chastity and a philosophy which believes love has the power to ennoble; at the same time we must also allow that the things of the flesh, outside the context of chastity, are deemed degenerate. Given today's mores, it is not unlikely numbers of people will find it difficult to appreciate the force of sexual jealousy any way near as potently as Othello or Iago. It is obviously true that the pronouncement, "Yet she must die, else she'll betray more men", is barbaric to us and yet not altogether unfamiliar when we read of present-day fundamentalist justice in some states but within the play's context it does, and needs to be seen to, arise out of character and conviction. Infidelity in the West has become a stock subject of sitcoms and a saleable commodity in newspapers. It is, in the words of Iago, a common thing. The experience the play has to offer can only be diminished if we do not understand infidelity as soul-destroying betrayal. This will also certainly be the case with other matters the play brings into debate: children's obedience to fathers, wives' obedience to husbands, the question of 'appetites', why honour should outlive honesty. It is important for us to realise that in this play no distinction is made between a crime and a sin. And, needless to say, our idea of 'nature' (conditioned as it largely is by the Romantics) would be foreign to the Elizabethans or Jacobeans, to whom it meant the whole cosmological setup and the known rules governing it. Behaviour contravening these was considered 'unnatural', a form of disobedience – in a word, sinful.

We need to have some knowledge of this orthodoxy if we are to appreciate the uneasinesses and scepticisms that also went into the making of the play. We need to know what is being reacted *against*. When Donne published his *An Anatomy of the World* in 1611 he declared that the old order had been called into doubt: he knew that the geocentric universe of Ptolemy and of the Church had been called into question by Copernicus, Giordano Bruno, Galileo:

> And new philosophy calls all in doubt,
> the element of fire is quite put out;
> The sun is lost, and th'earth, and no man's wit
> Can well direct him where to look for it ...
> ... 'Tis all in pieces, all coherence gone
> All just supply, and all relation.
> Prince, subject, father son are things forgot ...

In other words, long-held notions of order were collapsing and our modern world beginning.

With this play we have moved into a new century and, as is most often the case, it is a time of uncertainty rather than of hope – or a tremulous mixture of the two. Most commentators recognise a shift of mood as Shakespeare begins writing the tragedies – some foolishly attributing this to a change in Shakespeare's private affairs. In 1603, the year Shakespeare may have started writing *Othello*, Elizabeth I died childless; there was, among other things, the worrying question of the Succession, and the eventual crowning of a new monarch fuelling fears as to how the religious and political map of England would alter.

As the play is primarily an experience in language, we need to be sensitive to usages not our own. Part of the pleasure of engaging with Shakespeare is that the adjustments we keep making simply enrich our experience of listening in the theatre or reading. If Shakespeare is another country there is much to be gained from establishing friendly relations.

In many ways, truth and its exposure are central concerns of tragedy but we need to be on our guard when it comes to where truth may or may not be located. When characters speak we have always to remember the context in which they are doing so: whether what they say expresses truly what they think/feel/know or whether and to what degree they are responding to situations and saying what they want others to hear. It is not easy trying to live up to Edgar's words at the end of *King Lear*: that we should "speak what we feel, not what we ought to say". Soliloquies may or may not tell us the truth; the soliloquist may be drawing the audience into complicity – something Iago's prototype, Richard III, is master of. The soliloquies of villains like Iago feed our sneaking admiration for "clever devils" and indulge the secret wish they might finally get away with it (while all the while safely knowing they won't and don't). Hamlet's traditionally problematic soliloquies do not explain him to us, never mind explain him to himself. The only moment we may feel certain of truth is when a character is speaking in his or her dying moments or words are spoken of them just after they have died. Take Emilia's dying words for example:

> Moor, she was chaste; She loved thee, cruel Moor,
> So come my soul to bliss, as I speak true;
> So speaking as I think, I die, I die.

> (Act V, scene 2, 246-8)

Both audience and those on stage are meant to accept these words as crucially true.

The play may be seen as a competition between different kinds of language: heroic manly language (the so-called Othello music written about by G. Wilson Knight)) and the cynicism and profanities of the alehouse. Threading into this and complicating it is the language of courtly love, such as we find Cassio and Desdemona innocently yet dangerously using.

Because Elizabethan/Jacobean English is extraordinarily flexible, Shakespeare is able to exploit many kinds of verbal resonance; words, phrases echo and re-echo. We are constantly aware of ambiguity, of deadly-serious puns, words with multiple and sometimes even contradictory meanings: words like "blood", "hot", "moist", "honest" (William Empson has meticulously explored this word as used in the play), "honour", "fair", "free", "use", "perdition" – words which keep being repeated and which give the play its particular texture. For instance, Iago remembers Brabantio's "She has deceived her father and may thee" and repeats it at a telling moment in the drama where "deceived" now carries the extra weight of meaning to cuckold. Think how a verb like 'use' carries the sense of 'look after' in "Use her well, Moor" and has the meaning of unlawful sexual gratification in "That he hath used thee". Take this interchange between Cassio and Iago:

> Cassio   I have made bold, Iago, to send in to your wife;
> My suit to her is that she will to the virtuous Desdemona
> Procure me some access.
>
> Iago   I'll send her to you presently;
> And I'll devise a mean to draw the Moor
> Out of the way, that your converse and business
> May be more free.

(Act III, scene 1, 32-7)

The audience is aware of sinister puns at work here: "procure" is a word associated with bawds; "access" then takes on the idea of entrance into not just my lady's chamber but into my lady's sexual favour. Iago's words "business" and "free" continue the reference, with suggestions of sexual transaction and liberality. This is the way the language of this play likes to work. Words having a surface innocence but an undercurrent of additional and often sinister meanings. In a word, equivocation. It is part of the aim of Iago (and, again, part of the play's 'logic') to drag others down to his linguistic level: his barrack-room vulgarity trashing both heroic and courtly ways of speaking.

The sexual meaning the Elizabethans ascribed to the verb 'to die' (to experience orgasm) will be important to my interpretation of the 'logic' of the play.

... ...

What I'd like to do first is consider what I will call the texture of the play. But before doing so, let me say that my approach is not so much that of the academic critic but more in the spirit of someone setting up a hypothetical production. The things I say here are what I would want to discuss with the actors, in order, hopefully, to bring the play to life and make a sensible production of it. It is, as it were, one part of a script conference in which – it goes without saying – everything is up for discussion. With luck, we will avoid dogmatism if we understand that many seeming statements are actually questions in disguise. One only has to look at the diversity of opinion among critics to be put on one's guard: Bradley seeing Othello as heroic, accepting the Moor's own estimations of himself; Leavis challenging this to suggest that he is emotionally unstable; or the middle position taken by a critic like Robert Heilman, who sees Othello as heroic but profoundly flawed by pride and naivety. The best that can be hoped for is intelligent consensus.

This book is not a formal attempt to arrive at answers; it is best seen as a series of questionings – in which I have allowed intuition to play its part – of major issues the play raises. It is perhaps more a poet's eye-view than an academic's. The sections that follow consider the play in terms of dynamic tensions generated by sequences of opposites and go on to discuss Othello's 'credulity', the pervasiveness of the sanguine humour, the 'innocence' of Desdemona, Othello's over-reliance on absolutes, the real and unreal motivations of Iago, the importance of good name/reputation, what we are to understand of jealousy, Iago's methods, the so-called 'tragic flaw', the roles of Emilia and Bianca, the actions of kissing and touching, Othello's sense of justice and what view we take of him at the end of the play, the manifold references to Heaven and Hell, the business of speaking and not speaking, seeing and not seeing. In conclusion I suggest that the relationship between Othello and Iago may be a symbiotic one.

Books and articles referred to will be listed at the end.

2   Tensions Between Opposites

Othello is Shakespeare's only domestic tragedy with a contemporary setting. It has surprisingly little in the way of the legendary, folkloric or mythic about it. Most of its imagery is Christian and drawn from Heaven and Hell – which to most of its audience was neither fable nor poetic description but simply constituted its reality. Strictly speaking therefore, it is inaccurate to refer to it as imagery: what is poetic and metaphorical to us was to Shakespeare's audience more in the nature of allusion to invisible aspects of their reality. They are references rather than metaphors.

There is talk of witchcraft and magic, and Othello's Muslim background releases the imagination into suggestions of the exotic but on the whole the play is relatively naturalistic. We are encouraged to believe the actions arise out of 'real' conditions and happen to 'real' people. We have to allow for telescoping and dramatic shaping but are only aware of these when we step back analytically. When it is in motion we scarcely worry about what has been called 'double-time' (was there time for Cassio and Desdemona to have an illicit affair or even for Othello and Desdemona – something to be taken up later – to consummate their marriage?): the play's intensity and its modulations of pace ensure our willing suspension of disbelief. As Harley Granville-Barker has said:

> Shakespeare ... is not essentially concerned with time and the calendar at all. These, as with the actor and his behaviour ... must be given plausibility. But the play's essential action lies in the processes of thought and feeling by which the characters are moved and the story is forwarded. And the deeper the springs of these the less do time, place and circumstances affect them. His imagination is now concerned with fundamental passions, and its swift working demands unencumbered expression. He may falsify the calendar for his convenience but we shall find neither trickery nor anomaly in the fighting of the intellectual battle for Othello's soul. And in the light of the truth of this the rest will pass unnoticed.

In performance a terrible and terrifying 'logic' is in progress. What we are witnessing is a man on a collision course and the climax, when it comes, whether we can endure it or not, is something we are required to witness. In *Macbeth* the most important murder, that of Duncan, is committed off-stage: we know it has happened when Macbeth enters with bloodstained hands and daggers and the words "I have done the deed". In *Othello* we are witnesses and accomplices. *Macbeth* is a play about consequences and conscience. *Othello* takes us on an inexorable emotional journey towards a fatal end.

It is a nervy play, one which has a gathering intensity. Paralleling this, we have starkness and a claustrophobic feeling of increasing confinement. (It is of some real significance, as I hope to show, that Desdemona is smothered). We move from the darkness of a busy war-anxious Venice, from the street to a council chamber; then to an island – first to its quayside (having emerged from a storm) and then to its fortifications and finally into its Governor's bedroom with – in most performances I have seen – its curtained four-poster bed. What I am suggesting is that we keep moving into increasingly constricting settings. It is also a movement from public to private (or a confusing of the two), a homing-in on execution/murder.

There is a general starkness to the language. You have only to compare it with the poetic densities of *Macbeth*. In *Othello* we are made aware of the contrast between language heightened into poetry and language debased. It is part of the play's 'logic' that at one crucial point Othello ends up speaking disjointed prose, his language collapses altogether. Colours are either black or white or, more accurately, a confusion of black and white. What other colour there is stands out sharply from the general tone – the handkerchief spotted with strawberries (a pre-echo of the bed said to be "with lust's blood spotted"), the green of "green-eyed monster". Generally the language of the play is plain: when it is heightened we are aware that it is so. Patches of so-called comic relief are played down. Desdemona's catechism of Iago at the quayside in Cyprus produces no sparkle. "O most lame and impotent conclusion" she says and it is a judgement that the performance of Iago, as pseudo-clown, deserves. He is no Feste. A clown, so designated, does appear on two occasions. At the beginning of Act III one such comes on to tell Cassio that Othello doesn't like or is not in the mood for music, but his 'quillets' are obscene and leave a nasty taste. He is a poor, yet sinister echo of

Iago. In scene 4 of the same Act, the clown, this time sent by Desdemona to seek out Cassio, utters nothing but vulgar and jaded quips. The reason for this is that Shakespeare doesn't want to distract us too much by lessening the tension, breaking the spell, bringing us out from our willing suspension of disbelief. We jeer at this feeble clown rather than laugh with him. He too is no Feste, more a parodic version of Iago. This is not to ignore the point, made by David Gervais in his essay *The Comic Muse,* that to see the tragic nobility of Othello as purely that – i.e. excluding elements of the comic (the hero's propensity for making a fool of himself) – is to diminish the play's 'psychological acuity'. Gervais states that "to have made Othello *purely* tragic would have softened the tragedy and left us with something nobler and easier to bear". Shakespeare, that is, had the courage to draw upon the pettiness of comedy and make Othello "as ignorant as dirt" despite his "noble nature". In other words, the comic in this play is not simply a matter of scenes of comic relief but part of the general mix and therefore 'truer to life', nearer to general experience than the purities of classical tragedy.

So we have intensity, pace, and starkness. But more than any of this, our emotional and moral responses are conditioned by what I will call a patterning or sequencing of opposites. It is tension between these that energises the play and gives it its dynamism and its web of significances. The first and most obvious thing on view is Othello's blackness and Desdemona's European whiteness. We can no more ignore the Moor's blackness than we can Hamlet's inky cloak: these focus what we see on stage by standing out from the milieu they are found in. As Geoffrey Matthews says:

> The most important feature of Othello is the colour of his skin. This is superficially obvious enough, but most critics have avoided treating Othello's colour as the essence of the play for two good reasons: first it is unhistorical to suppose that 'colour' as we understand the term, had much meaning for the Elizabethans or early Jacobeans; and second, that to interpret Othello as a play about race would be like saying that Henry VI is a play about fatness ... (With Elizabethan audiences) the unfamiliarity of the colour-problem would even tend to increase its impact: the marriage between Othello and Desdemona must have been very startling to an audience that

had never seen coloured boy walking out with a white girl. Professor Dover Wilson goes further and says: 'If anyone imagines that England was unconscious of the "colour-bar", they cannot have read Othello with any care.'

Almost everything in the play focuses on this contrasting black/ white relationship. Black in the case of Hamlet shows him to be the only one at court properly observing the proprieties of mourning the recent death of the king, his father, while everyone else is either wilfully ignoring or has been coerced into ignoring this sacramental duty; Othello's blackness is problematic in another way: black is the colour of the Devil, Hell and sin. Shakespeare is asking his audience if black can be noble and good. It is an obvious irony, as Eldred Jones rightly points out, that it is Iago who "reproduces and exaggerates many of the unfavourable characteristics commonly credited to Moors".

... ...

Things are put into uneasy nervous relationships. Tension and confusion are essential ingredients in the dramatic suspense. The play opens with panic, intrigue, disorder, loud shouting, obscenities, torches, fear, hate (the keynote of hatred is sounded three times within the first seven lines). Then there is the drunken brawl in Cyprus crucially interrupting Othello's wedding night:

> Why, how now, ho! From whence ariseth this?
> Are we turned Turks, and to ourselves do that
> Which heaven hath forbid the Ottomites?
> For Christian shame put by this barbarous brawl!

> (Act II, scene 3, 168-171)

Confusion is perhaps easiest to illustrate in the reports of the Turkish manoeuvres brought before the Venetian Council: 107 galleys are first mentioned, then 140, then 200; then no-one is sure whether they are heading for Cyprus or for Rhodes, that is until information arrives that the Turks have gone to Rhodes to meet up with "an after fleet" of some 30 more ships. Right into the middle of this war council strides a domestic crisis: the man in charge of the action has eloped with a senator's daughter.

The storm that bangs the Turkish fleet too is emblematic of confusion and disorder: it "seems to cast water on the burning Bear/ And quench the guards of th' ever-fixèd Pole." It is emblematic of the emotional storm to come; it is also dramatically purposeful. It denies Othello victory by doing the job for him. It is, so to speak, an act of God. Through this, Shakespeare regulates the amount of glory Othello can lay claim to, simply because he wants us to see him for what he is rather than for what he has done. Here we have another instance in Shakespeare of the man of action on shaky ground in a civil/domestic setting, ill-equipped to play the moth of peace. Macbeth is such another, a man splendid on the battlefield but given to fear and anxiety at home. By the same token, we have in Iago a soldier maybe as ruthless on the battlefield as Macbeth, (" … in the trade of war I have slain men") but determined on mischief in a civil situation and in people's private lives. He is a familiar figure in Elizabethan and Jacobean drama: the malcontent, the cynic-soldier, out of boredom creating civil intrigue.

He is not, however, a melodramatic villain (though I have seen at least one performance where he was more Richard III than Iago) but a plausible being, a twenty-eight-year-old Venetian with a real set of self-justifications. He is not nor was meant to be a ham actor.

The above are fairly obvious instances of confusion and tension – tension between what seems and what actually is the truth. And this is of course a major theme in Shakespeare's plays: conflict and tension between appearance and reality – a constant theme, one perhaps not unnatural to a writer whose job is to lie artistically, to *feign*. As Touchstone tells us in *As You Like It*: "the truest poetry is the most feigning." It is not without significance that a contemporary word for actor was 'shadow'. There is a real frisson in *King Lear* when the king, asked to identify himself, answers that he is "Lear's shadow".

Some indication of the Renaissance idea of man's position and role in the universe might be helpful here. It is put concisely by George Herbert in his poem *Affliction IV* when he describes man as:

> A wonder tortured in the space
> Betwixt this world and that of grace.

This in itself would provide a fine epitaph for all of Shakespeare's tragic heroes and heroines. Man understood as a paradigm of the tensions between the sublunary world, that part of God's creation below the moon, subject to Mutability ... Time, Death and decay ... and the superlunary regions of the Cosmos. Halfway between the angels and the beasts, his bestial or corporal nature is subject to corruption occasioned by Original Sin; his higher nature, his soul, his mind, his reason are attributes he shares with the angels and which lift him towards Heaven; through their proper exercise he may attain redemption, grace and eternal life.

Cassio summarises the 'logic' of the play when, after the corrupting influence of drink, he says in Act II, scene 3, "To be now a sensible man, by and by a fool, and presently a beast."

(We should note that drink is referred to in the play as "the devil drink".)

Cassio's statement is simple logic; it is the 'logic' of the play. Corrupt a man's mind and you reduce him to the level of the beasts; taint his reason and you send him mad and put him on the path to perdition. Iago is recognised as both beast (viper, dog) and devil at the play's end. Images of bestiality – toads, goats, monkeys, horses, asses, rams, sometimes with their accompanying smells ("one may smell in her a will most rank") and suggestions of slime ("the slime/ That sticks on filthy deeds") – are woven again and again into its fabric.

... ...

Whenever I see or read the play I am invariably reminded of Blake's "two contrary states of the human soul" and, in particular, his poem, *The Sick Rose*:

> O Rose thou art sick.
> The invisible worm,
> That flies in the night
> In the howling storm:
>
> Has found out thy bed
> Of crimson joy:
> And his dark secret love
> Does thy life destroy.

This would make an even more appropriate epitaph for the tragic love of Othello and Desdemona. Equally, it reflects very pertinently on the relationship between the Moor and Iago. But for the moment let's just register it as underlining the idea of life interpreted in terms of opposites and the dynamic relationship between them. Man the paradoxical creature tortured in the space betwixt this world and that of grace.

Consider the war between Venice and the Ottomites. This is a fundamental tension of opposites. What we have is a rich merchant republic, relying on foreign mercenaries, a Moor as top brass with his newly-promoted Florentine lieutenant – both resented by the native-born Venetian Iago – to defend its shipping-routes against the might of the Turkish Empire. This sets the whole known world in opposition: Christian and Infidel, Godly and Ungodly, Truth and Untruth, white western civilisation and coloured oriental barbarism: rich sophisticated Renaissance Venice and pagan barbaric Turkey. Othello is, at the moment in time that is the play, a pivot on which this division of the known world into two mighty opposing camps rests. In the eyes of its first audiences it is the unequivocal opposition of right and wrong.

This established, it is not difficult to see the same opposing forces activating and directing Othello's character. He is baptised a Christian (in Act II scene 3 Iago uses the words "were't to renounce his baptism") and Othello certainly has most of the Christian language in the play; but he is by birth a heathen Moor or Muslim. He still has, despite his conversion, the primitive and pagan in him. And Iago, knowing this, studies and exposes it – "Men should be what they seem". Traditionally, too, Moors were held to be naturally hot-blooded, more so than most. Cassio's choleric nature is tame by comparison. In addition, Othello has a certain exotic quality in his character, an exciting and seductive kind of mystique. What else did Desdemona fall for? And her father before her? We see that he is sometimes superstitious (in his valuation of the handkerchief for instance); and, above all, he is a black among whites, an extravagant and wheeling stranger. Our current sympathies and political attitudes tend to make us, in modern performances, focus perhaps rather exclusively on this aspect of the play, to see it as an exposé of racism. This is not to deny this aspect its importance. It is, however, one facet of a multi-facetted dramatic experience.

Othello's lately-acquired Christianity and his pagan background can be made to go to war within him. Men should be what they seem. Iago indeed makes it his task – as if set on revealing an hypocrisy – to expose the 'real' man to himself and the world.

It is not unreasonable to suppose and suggest that Othello has *chosen* the world of European Christian civilisation in which to make his way – an ambitious man who, as an outsider, wants to be accepted and respected in Venice. Yet, all of this, like his colour, gives him an on-stage uniqueness and a potential vulnerability. In the eyes of Iago he is ripe for picking.

He is content and secure in positions of power and, as luck will have it, he has soldierly qualities that Venice is desperately in need of: he is the man of the moment, with a proven track record as a military hero (see for example Montano's later estimation of him in Act II, scene 1, 35-6), and it is this that initially protects and in the long run exposes him. He is, as we have said, a convert to Christianity and has run off with the much-sought-after daughter of a leading Venetian citizen. (Could he be said to be betraying his racial origins in doing so? The Venetians assume he is betraying their code of conduct). We also know that he is getting on in years. In Act III scene 3 he confesses "I am declined/ Into the vale of years". It is not too fanciful to imagine a man taking early retirement and settling down where the living is good – a resented outsider with an insecurity to be exposed. If this isn't so, why the elopement? Is this why he projects himself as self-controlled and made of the best heroic mettle? In order to impress and therefore be accepted in Venice? Or is it simply that his self-image is limited to his experience and his consequent view of himself as a soldier employed in the honourable business of 'glorious war', dependant for his being on military heroism? Is he innocent or ignorant of the ways of the world, especially a world as sophisticated as the one Venetians inhabit and he has married into? Is he too, like Iago, a gambler? Marrying the fair Desdemona, expecting to be Venice's hero, Governor of Cyprus (the glory he could claim of victory, as we've said, is denied him by the storm and, in any case, once the security of Cyprus is made certain, the state simply calls him home, deputing Cassio in his place). The answer is surely all of these things. In the way that Lady Macbeth leans on her husband by casting doubt on his valour and, by implication, his sexual potency, so Iago knows what it means for men to appear or be made to appear unmanly. He describes Othello's epileptic fit (the collapse of his reason) to Cassio (who has witnessed it) as "a passion most unsuiting in a man".

Othello, always dangerously, tends to see things in absolute terms ("When I love thee not,/ Chaos is come again"); it can be argued, and without cynicism, that he gambles on Venice and loses his chips, a wager in which he forfeits a pearl richer than all his tribe. The love he declares for Desdemona can also be seen as a dangerous (dangerous when men like Iago are listening) form of dependence:

> If it were now to die,
> 'Twere now to be most happy; for I fear
> My soul hath her content so absolute
> That not another comfort like to this
> Succeeds in unknown fate.

(Act II, scene 1, 187-191)

These lines had a profound impact on Keats when he came to write his *Ode to a Nightingale*. What they reveal of Othello is a divided nature. They smack more of infatuation – either that or as revealing uncertainty – than love. No wonder Desdemona protests:

> The heavens forbid
> But that our loves and comforts should increase,
> Even as our days do grow.

(Act II, scene 1, 192-4)

Iago is listening to what might not unreasonably be thought of as a man publicly expressing not love but a form of extreme attachment to a particular idea of self. Do we consider this naive or innocent? Whatever it is, Iago cannot resist: it is a sporting challenge, a test to destruction, and Iago, being Iago, would be denying his own nature if he didn't rise to it, "practising upon his peace and quiet,/ Even to madness". A lion does not walk past a lamb; a Mephistopheles doesn't walk away from Faustus. John Wain aptly compares Othello to "some huge man-of-war, aground in a creek, an easy prey to a boarding party in a rowing boat".

It can be argued that Othello, keen to be respected, hungry for honour and eager for the security and the certainties that Christian Venice – despite its own vulnerabilities (it is after all beset by a mighty enemy) – seems to afford him, is unconsciously prepared to accept his undoing – as soldiers are prepared to accept death as part of the job description.

It is important to know too that generals are required to make snap decisions ("once to be in doubt is once to be resolved") and at all times prefer death to dishonour. Consider how quickly suicide comes into his mind:

> Her name, that was as fresh
> As Dian's visage, is now begrimed and black
> As mine own face. If there be cords or knives
> Poison or fire or suffocating streams,
> I'll not endure it.

> (Act III, scene 3, 383-7)

(Note in passing the word "suffocating" and also that Othello thinks of his reputation/honour first. And note too that, in Shakespeare, there are two attitudes to suicide: (1) that those who commit it go automatically to Hell (2) that it can be an honourable exit for a soldier to fall, after the Roman fashion, onto his sword).

If we do not recognise honour as the driving force in Othello's life we will not understand him. Once we do, we can perhaps allow that the major conflict that arises in him – exacerbated by Iago's machinations – is between the will to live and the escape death provides. To be or not to be.

Othello has been a soldier all his life and confesses to be getting on in years. In the Council Chamber he tells the senators:

> Rude am I in my speech,
> And little blessed with the soft phrase of peace;
> For since these arms of mine had seven years' pith,
> Till now some nine moons wasted, they have used
> Their dearest action in the tented field;

And little of this great world can I speak
More than pertains to feats of broil and battle;

(Act I, scene 3, 81-7)

From the age of seven, he suggests, he has known only war and even makes the point that he has "wasted" the last nine months waiting to be engaged in military action. (He has of course spent some of the time courting). What he is admitting is that he is a soldier not a citizen. All his life he has, presumably, moved in an all-male world (though we may still imagine camp followers), a world dedicated to the pursuit of honour, the "Pride, pomp, and circumstances of glorious war". And being a commander, his job is to make decisions which will quickly eradicate uncertainty. The decisions we see him taking in the play are all concerned with the determination to remove uncertainty. They reveal his training and experience as a soldier; they also reveal a measure of nervousness in a civil situation and in domestic life. Witness his peremptory dismissal of Cassio:

Cassio, I love thee,
But nevermore be officer of mine.

(Act II, scene 3, 247-8)

Notice how this is affected by the sudden appearance at this point of Desdemona:

Look, if my gentle love be not raised up.
I'll make thee an example.

(Act II, scene 3, 248-9)

Again, this is the soldier talking, determined at all costs be seen to keep up a proper dignity.

He is the admirable poised warrior when he comes face to face with Brabantio in Act I scene 2:

> Keep up your bright swords, for the dew will rust them.
> Good signior, you shall more command with years
> Than with your weapons.

(Act I, scene 2, 59-61)

He is modest, sane and in command before the Duke. However, in Cyprus, representing civil authority, confronting and sorting out brawls between his friends and associates, he is seen to fluster and to express powerful and dangerous emotions he has so far tried to keep in check:

> Now, by heaven,
> My blood begins my safer guides to rule,
> And passion, having my best judgement collied,
> Assays to lead the way. Zounds, if I stir,
> Or do but lift this arm, the best of you
> Shall sink in my rebuke.

(Act II, scene 3, 204-9)

This is a military voice not the voice of civil justice. The voice of civil justice is that of the Duke of Venice; Othello's idea of justice is that of a General. Whenever he thinks his honour is under attack he accepts the circumstances as 'destiny', as an essential feature of a soldier's life, as later he is to see cuckoldry as part of this destiny:

> Yet 'tis the plague of great ones;
> Prerogatived are they less than the base.
> 'Tis destiny unshunnable, like death:

(Act III, scene 3, 273-5)

This is a man used to facing extremities, now aware, both in Venice and Cyprus, that he is uncomfortably 'different' and is not going to be allowed to have his cake and eat it.

Among the contraries in operation in this play are:

Christian/Infidel
Civilisation/Barbarism
White/Black
Professional/Domestic
Innocence/Experience
Storm/Calm
Love/Duty
Passion/Reason
Language Heightened/ Language Debased
Self-love/Selflessness
Chastity/Promiscuity
Wit/Witchcraft
Soul/Body

Venice/Ottomite
Angel/Devil
Public/Private
Youth/Age
Love/Hate
Honour/Disgrace
Imagination/Reason
Man/Beast
Poetry/Prose
Love/Lust
Virtue/Vice
Sacrifice/Murder
Life/Death

3   Fair in Love and War

On the question of Othello's blackness, Anthony Holden interestingly suggests that Shakespeare would have known about Moors because of the visit of the Moorish ambassador of the King of Barbary to Elizabeth's court 1600-1. Holden reproduces the portrait of the turbanned ambassador painted during the visit and quotes Honigmann, the editor of the 1997 Arden edition of the play, as asking "Is it too fanciful to suppose that this very face haunted Shakespeare's imagination and inspired the writing of his tragedy?" Holden also suggests that he must have read John Leo's *A Geographical History of Africa* translated into English in 1600. Leo was himself a Moor with this to say of his countrymen: "No nation in the world is so subject unto jealousy, for they will rather lose their lives than put up any disgrace in the behalf of their women." They are "very proud and high-minded, and wonderfully addicted to wrath ... Their wits are but mean, and they are so credulous that they will believe matters impossible which are told them." (Holden also cites Pliny as the source of Othello's speech about his adventures that so impressed Desdemona).

Whatever the truth of this, we will need to think about the word 'credulous' when we come to make a final judgement on Othello. For the moment let's see him as a complex character, not a stereotype, and suggest he is neither weak nor stupid nor gullible. You have only to compare him with Roderigo, who *is* stupid and gullible. With a gullible character, poetic justice comes into play: you are simply glad to see comeuppance meted out. Nor is Othello a cardboard character representing a hollow kind of nobility, even if I seem to put honour at the centre as his driving force and, like Iago, have seemed to undermine it. It is too easy to focus attention – both in text and performance – on Iago, who, in the theatre, invariably holds most of our attention. But Othello is many times the man Iago is. If he seeks integration into Christianity and Western civilisation we are meant to see this as his choosing the good and true things of life.

The real tragedy is that the love between Othello and Desdemona had no chance to increase with the years. Othello wants to be part, to accept and understand the moral, religious and social customs of a civilisation radically different from anything he has previously known, and is ultimately not allowed to embrace. Because of uncertainty and his ignorance (or is it innocence?) of the ways of this world, his poise can be easily disturbed. So committed is he – having gambled his all (not wisely but too well) – that he believes in the end he has no avenue of retreat except the one offered by death. It is to his credit and part of his tragedy that he can resist only as far as he learns the true nature of his actions and his particular limitations will allow. We should never lose sight of the fact that he believes himself at all times to be an honourable man trying to maintain an essential dignity under great stress. He is vulnerable and corruptible. This tragedy plays out yet again a parallel with the realities of Original Sin.

We measure Othello's tragedy – as we do with other tragic heroes and heroines – by the quality of his suffering ("wrought in the extreme"). At the end of the play, judgement is not altogether ours – because of our complicity. We recognise the pity of it but judgement belongs in another court; it is that same judgement to which he wishes Desdemona to be subjected when he says:

> I would not kill thy unprepared spirit;
> No – heaven forfend! – I would not kill thy soul.

> (Act V, scene 2, 31-2)

He is a man wounded by the fact that virtue can apparently so easily and precipitously fall from grace, something he finds virtually impossible to believe. The fact is he never stops loving his wife, the fair Desdemona.

4   A Sense of Humour

In *Macbeth* blood is *physically* present; the play is steeped in it. Its first human words are "What bloody man is that?" as a wounded messenger comes in with report of an extremely bloody battle. There are bloody daggers, gashes, reeking purple wounds, bloody hands. In *Othello*, though there are woundings and killings, we are much more aware of blood as a humour.

Renaissance ideas about man's place in the universe and about the physical make-up of everything in it were very different to ours. An over-simple summary might run like this: what exists below the moon is made up of four elements: earth, water, air and fire. The last three of these exist as spheres between earth and the moon. The mixture, being imperfect (as opposed to the immutable perfections of God's creation beyond the moon), was subject to the processes of time, decay and death. A pure balance of elements was nowhere to be found in the sublunary regions. The moon itself is frequently referred to as inconstant, changeable, an exciter of madness (or *lunacy*): it has particular influence over lovers, as we see, say, in *A Midsummer Night's Dream*. The spheres above the moon evince the qualities of the Divinity: constancy and harmony. Man, at the centre of the universe and the pinnacle of earthly creation, was, like everything else, made up of the four elements in imperfect mixtures. As the mixture varied from person to person so it was thought to determine character. This gave rise to the theory of four basic psychological types. A preponderance of earth created the melancholy man; water produced the phlegmatic type; fire produced choler and hot-temper; air produced blood or the sanguine humour. It is this last which dominates *Othello*.

Notice it is associated with air. Mention has already been made of something claustrophobic at work in the play, the idea of increasingly constricting settings. Smell makes us aware of air or the lack of it and it is not without significance, as we have said, that Desdemona is suffocated.

The humour blood was said to be hot and moist. Now we can see the significance of phrases like "hot as monkeys"; why Desdemona's hand is referred to as a "sweating devil":

This argues fruitfulness and liberal heart.
Hot, hot, and moist. This hand of yours requires
A sequester from liberty. fasting and prayer,
Much castigation, exercise devout;
For there's a young and sweating devil here
That commonly rebels. 'Tis a good hand,
A frank one.

(Act III, scene 4, 38-44)

It is the humour responsible for exciting the sexual passions ("the beast with two backs") and the devil wrath. Iago utters received wisdom when he tells Roderigo "If the beam of our lives had not one scale of reason to poise another of sensuality, the blood and baseness of our natures would conduct us to most preposterous conclusions. But we have reason to cool our raging motions, our carnal stings, our unbitted lusts." He is not to be thought wrong in these sentiments; it is the relish with which he utters them that makes us suspect there is more to it for him than a rehearsal of truisms. There is a deep cynicism at work. And of course it is characteristic of the man to confuse love with lust. He calls love "a lust of the blood and a permission of the will." Notice that the word "blood" is present in both quotations. Later he is to tell Roderigo that Desdemona will eventually become sexually disenchanted with Othello "when the blood is made dull with the act of sport." Passion devours the reason, it eats up. The first blow to Othello's poise causes him to say "My blood begins my safer guides to rule."

Brabantio assumes that Othello has excited his daughter's blood with drugs or charms. The humour blood is frightening transformed into the idea of real blood in Othello's line "Thy bed, lust-stained, shall be with lust's blood spotted" – a cruel parody of the droit de seigneur moment sheets are publicly exhibited to prove a woman is no longer virgo intacta. When Desdemona notices how wrought her husband is before killing her she says:

Why gnaw you so your nether-lip?
Some bloody passion shakes your very frame:

(Act V, scene 2, 43-4)

These examples indicate how important this highly volatile humour is to our understanding of the play. The word 'blood' has many meanings: among them ancestry and nobility and also, in opposition, passion, animal nature.

5 My Life upon her Faith

In sonnet 116 Shakespeare writes:

> Let me not to the marriage of true minds
> Admit impediments, love is not love
> Which alters when it alteration findes,
> Or bends with the remover to remove.
> O no, it is an ever fixèd marke
> That looks on tempests and is never shaken;
> It is the star to every wandering barke,
> Whose worths unknown, although his higth be taken.
> Love's not Times foole, though rosie lips and cheeks
> Within his bending sickles compasse come,
> Love alters not with his breefe houres and weekes,
> But beares it out even to the edge of doome:
>   If this be error and upon me proved,
>   I never writ, nor no man ever loved.

Standing before the Council requesting Desdemona be given leave to go to Cyprus, Othello makes this assertion:

> Vouch with me, heaven, I therefore beg it not
> To please the palate of my appetite,
> Nor to comply with heat – the young affects
> In me defunct – and proper satisfaction;
> But to be free and bounteous to her mind.

(Act I, scene 3, 256-260)

In other words, he believes he's old enough (and it is a fault of some productions to make him look younger than he is) not to be troubled by sexual cravings or at least that he can handle them. She makes a similar claim when she says "I saw Othello's visage in his mind".

If we apply the philosophy of love we find in the sonnet, then what both Othello and Desdemona say is meant to draw serious approval. In the Council Chamber one of the senators asks whether Desdemona's affection for Othello

came ... by request and such fair question
As soul to soul affordeth?

(Act I, scene 3, 113-4)

The question implies an orthodoxy in which love is a matter of mind to mind, soul to soul.

Love then is – ideally – a marriage of true *minds* and not simply of sexual compatibilities. Love's theme is constancy – an aspiration, an emulation of that quality which is the dominant feature of the heavenly spheres above the moon. It does not alter when it alteration finds. It has claims on immortality, bears it out even to the edge of doom, the Day of Judgement. As the stars are chaste, so chastity is to be prized: it is heavenly, as carnal stings and unbitted lusts are hellish. ("Unbitted" suggesting horses out of control).

In *Othello* the declarations both the Moor and Desdemona make are perhaps best seen as expressions of faith and good intention rather than the statements of people who understand what their sudden marriage is based on and requires.

Let's not forget that their marriage is an elopement and therefore undertaken without a father's permission, never mind his blessing. Does it presuppose Othello would not get such blessing? If, not – given Brabantio's familiarity with him – it is worth asking why not. It is secret, underhand and 'unnatural'. Desdemona's father cannot believe it hasn't been brought about without the aid of charms and drugs:

O thou foul thief! Where hast thou stowed my daughter?
Damned as thou art, thou hast enchanted her:

(Act I, scene 2, 61-2)

And later to the Duke:

She is abused, stolen from me, and corrupted
By spells and medicines bought of mountebanks;

(Act I, scene 3, 60-1)

to which the Duke replies:

25

> Whoe'er he be that in this foul proceeding
> Hath thus beguiled your daughter of herself
> And you of her, the bloody book of law
> You shall yourself read in the bitter letter
> After your own sense; yea, though our proper son
> Stood in your action.

(Act I, scene 3, 65-9)

These are the reactions of highly-placed powerful people representing law and justice – in a word, orthodoxy within the play. The audience is torn between concurring and sympathy for the lovers.

The marriage is a mixture of races and customs deemed by this orthodoxy to be 'unnatural'. Othello, later remembering things said in the Council Chamber, hears himself, in Act II, scene 3, echoing Brabantio: "And yet, how nature erring from itself."

Iago in reply also cunningly echoes (as a form of confirmation) Brabantio's sentiments:

> Ay, there's the point: as, to be bold with you,
> Not to affect many proposèd matches
> Of her own clime, complexion, and degree,
> Whereto we see in all things nature tends,
> Foh! One may smell in such a will most rank,
> Foul disproportion, thoughts unnatural.

(Act III, scene 3, 228-233)

(Note the emphasis on bad smells).

Moreover, the sudden marriage/elopement could hardly be more badly timed. What a time to choose for a wedding and a honeymoon! Othello's military skills and duties are in urgent demand and, as a man whose self-confessed experience has been all on the battlefield, he is suddenly importing into his life all kinds of unknown and potentially bewildering things. Add to that the fact that he is ignorant (innocent?) of 'civilised' Venetian behaviour. Once Iago has infected Othello's ear, it is easy enough for him to insinuate and expect some acquiescence:

I know our country disposition well:
In Venice they do let god see the pranks
They dare not show their husbands; their best conscience
Is not to leave't undone, but kept unknown.

(Act III, scene 3, 199-202)

The incredulous Moor asks "Dost thou say so?" and from thereon is truly snared!

And then of course when we first meet Desdemona with her talk of "downright violence, and storm of fortunes" we may be tempted to wonder whether he has met his soulmate and/or is taking on a rather determined woman.

What is meant to be a spiritual union of two souls now, on the face of it, looks to be ill-timed and ill-considered. Is it enough for Othello to say, because Desdemona seriously inclined to listen to his tales of adventure, that he "loved her that she did pity them"? Is this really a marriage of true minds? Maybe it is a relationship meant to be seen inpotential or, in the light of events, as too good for this world, a world with such people as Iago in it. Or, yet again, as a disaster – Iago notwithstanding – bound to happen anyway, already containing the seeds of its own destruction?

On top of this Othello has made one of his officers (up until this point?) resentful by promoting a theoretician over him and ignoring the personal suit three great ones of the city made on his behalf. The question has to be asked: has Othello wrongly appointed Cassio? Was it for the services rendered as a go-between in the courtship? With hindsight we might well say that Othello wrongly appointed him: when they become aware of his 'unmanly' weaknesses his fellow soldiers automatically think the Moor should be told of an officer who has "unhappy brains for drinking" – a fault in him which actually leads to a brawl, to the collying of Othello's best judgement, and Cassio's summary dismissal.

6   A Maid so Tender, Fair and Happy

We are given distorted information about Othello and Desdemona (though we can only know this with hindsight) before we meet them and hear them speak for themselves. Our preconditioned views require modification. However, the earlier pictures remain in the back of our minds as a set of question marks. Before we meet him, Othello's name is blackened: having made one of his officers resentful over promotion, we ask how true is Iago's accusation that:

> 'Tis the curse of service:
> Preferment goes by letter and affection,
> And not by the old gradation, where each second,
> Stood heir to the first?

> (Act I, scene 1, 35-38)

Has the Moor peremptorily broken with tradition, custom, the law of nature? Has he again made a wrong judgement? And doesn't Iago give out similar reasons for expecting promotion to those his master gives him for marrying Desdemona? Iago claims a reputation based upon experience. He tells Roderigo:

> And I, of whom his eyes had seen the proof
> At Rhodes, at Cyprus, and on other grounds
> Christian and heathen ...

> (Act I, scene 1, 28-30)

Othello, warned by Iago that Brabantio will have the law on him, replies:

> Let him do his spite:
> My services, which I have done the signory
> Shall out-tongue his complaints. 'Tis yet to know –
> Which, when I know that boasting is an honour,
> I shall profulgate – I fetch my life and being
> From men of royal siege, and my demerits

May speak unbonneted to as proud a fortune
As this I have reached.

(Act I, scene 2, 18-25)

The word "fortune" echoes Roderigo's:

What a full fortune does the thick-lips owe
If he carry it thus!

(Act I, scene 1, 63-4)

where it stands for either great luck or substantial dowry or both.

At the start of the play Desdemona is presented to us as a white ewe being tupped by an old black ram and as someone who has made:

a gross revolt
Tying her duty, beauty, wit, and fortunes
In an extravagant and wheeling stranger
Of here and everywhere.

(Act I, scene 1, 131-4)

So what we expect of her and the Moor is for others to be outraged at their behaviour. This we see clearly in the reactions of her father and the Duke.

But then Othello famously persuades the Council in speeches that are assured, courteous, noble, and has them backed by similar speeches of Desdemona whom he requests be sent for with the words:

I do beseech you,
Send for the lady to the Sagittary
And let her speak of me before her father.
If you do find me foul in her report,
The trust, the office, I do hold of you
Not only take away, but let your sentence
Even fall upon my life.

(Act I, scene 3, 115-121)

We cannot fail to notice in these lines a preparedness to sacrifice life for dishonesty. It is a characteristic of tragedies that choice between all and nothing is frequently invoked. As Ibsen's eponymous Brand says, "compromise is the very devil" and then strides up the icy mountain declaiming "All or Nothing!" The same concepts lie at the heart of *Oedipus Rex* and *King Lear.* We are, of course, left at the end of such plays wondering which of these alternatives has been gained – all or nothing. Othello is another protagonist set against compromise.

He wins over the Duke and senators with his fine speeches. Do these, now that we have met the man, truly represent him as a man of honour and authority? Weren't we expecting "bombast circumstance/ Horribly stuffed with epithets of war"? Shakespeare's audiences may well have been expecting the stock figure of the braggart soldier only to be surprised by what now sounds like plausible nobility.

Desdemona comes on to stage for the first time with all the self-possession of her new husband. Her speeches suggest a strong-willed woman. The impact of her first speech causes her father to say despairingly:

> God be with you. I have done.
> Please it your Grace, on to the state affairs.
> I'd rather to adopt a child than get it.

(Act I, scene 3, 188-190)

It doesn't fit his picture of the perfect daughter, the modesty:

> in spite of nature,
> Of years, of country, credit, everything,
> To fall in love with that she feared to look on!

(Act I, scene 3, 96-8)

And when she declares:

> That I did love the Moor to live with him,
> My downright violence, and storm of fortunes
> May trumpet to the world. My heart's subdued

Even to the very quality of my lord.
I saw Othello's visage in his mind

(Act I, scene 3, 243-7)

she sounds like the "fair warrior" she is to be called later – not only
wanting to accompany her husband into the arena of war but also
determined on "the rites for why I love him", the consummation of
the marriage, which will make it absolute. It is interesting that Othello
immediately assures everyone that sex – the palate of his appetite,
complying with heat – is not a problem. Here again we have
protestations that he has everything under control, that ostensibly
what he and Desdemona have is a marriage of true minds. It is of
course what the senators need to hear of the man appointed to defend
them against the might of the Ottomites. Whether it is good news to
Desdemona is another question. We must wait to find out just how
strong-willed this woman really is.

In Act III scene 3, Iago cunningly echoes much of what we hear
in the Council Chamber. But in fact it is Othello, as we have already
noticed, who first sets up an echo of Brabantio with his line "And
yet, how nature erring from itself – " providing Iago with the perfect
cue:

Aye, there's the point, as (to be bold with you)
Not to affect many proposed matches
Of her own clime, complexion, and degree,
Whereto we see in all things nature tends –
Foh! one may smell in such a will most rank

(Act III, scene 3, 228-233)

something he could not have said earlier, but which now has, as we
have said, the ring of confirmation to it.

But what of Desdemona in the rest of the play?

7   Hail to Thee, Lady!

Act II begins with happy reunions after separations in an unusually ferocious storm, a "high-wrought flood". Shakespeare is careful in the ordering of arrivals ashore. Cassio is the first, separated from his master and earnestly praying for his safety. His expressions of loyalty we accept as heartfelt and we find them confirmed in Montano's regard for the noble Moor. Montano has served with him ("the man commands/ Like a full soldier") and admires him. The audience is now ready to reject Iago's estimation and regard him more as a hero. Not absolutely, not without reservation.

Cassio, the "proper man", eulogises Desdemona in terms appropriate to a courtier; he is well-bred with good manners and uses language that smacks of courtly love. Does he, we may ask, sound like a soldier, the man to be Othello's lieutenant? Perhaps we are meant to think he is laying it on thick, parading an over-refined politeness; we may even suspect that he may love the lady himself. Iago wants to think so. And he may be more than right in calling him an "arithmetician". It is a further instance of surface innocence masking – to sceptical ears –an exploitable naivety.

Next to arrive is not the Moor but Desdemona, accompanied by Iago and Emilia. This is our first glimpse of Iago's wife. Cassio continues in the same eulogistic vein but now it is within Iago's hearing. He talks of "our great captain's captain", a phrase that on the surface means that Othello has achieved his perfect partner but carries with it the suggestion that he is mastered by a woman, albeit a paragon, one who even influenced the tempest by virtue of her beauty. She is the "divine Desdemona". And before we know where we are he is comparing her to the Virgin Mary and ordering everyone to bend the knee:

> Hail to thee, lady! And the grace of heaven,
> Before, behind thee, and on every hand,
> Enwheel thee round.

> (Act II, scene 1, 85-7)

The parody of *Ave Maria* is inescapable. The picture Cassio gives is of a woman protected by heaven's grace. The dramatic irony of this is also inescapable.

Cassio continues (for example in Act II, scene 3) to use courtly terms to describe Desdemona. She is "a most exquisite lady", "a most fresh and delicate creature" and in Act III, scene 1 she is "the virtuous Desdemona". Iago, later cunningly confirming Cassio's picture of her, assures the cashiered lieutenant that she "is of so free, so kind, so apt, so blessed a disposition she holds it a vice in her goodness not to do more than she is requested" and is therefore the perfect candidate to intercede for him, as he now, with his courtly lover's language, is the perfect foil for Iago's mischief. We may note here an ironic reversal of roles and the suggestion that she too can be manipulated.

At the Cyprus quayside, Desdemona is properly anxious for her husband. Everyone else has arrived but him, and there is dramatic significance in the fact that he comes in last of all. But before he does, we have Cassio welcoming Iago's wife, Emilia, and kissing her – he protests – out of good manners. The cynical joke (and it is not without sexual innuendo) that Iago utters in reply:

> Sir, would she give you so much of her lips
> As of her tongue she oft bestows on me,
> You'd have enough.

(Act II, scene 1, 100-2)

launches him into a tirade against women. Depending on how we decide to stage this (allowing the women to overhear or requiring Iago to take Cassio aside), we can either see this as playful teasing, a kind of conventional mockery, an diversion to pass the time, or as a form of men's talk. It is perhaps a pseudo-humorous mask (Venice is the place of masks): Iago the hen-pecked husband! Desdemona, not impressed, sees through it all, without fully realising what it is she sees, when she says of his sentiments "These are old fond paradoxes to make fools laugh i' th' alehouse." Exactly so. If men should be what they seem, this is Iago being just that. "O most lame and impotent conclusion" is her judgement ... and the word "impotent" should give us pause. In his attitude to women Iago is exposed as a shallow fool. This, it can be argued, is almost certainly a measure of hatred towards them.

Cassio, again not realising the full weight of his words, ever polite, tells Desdemona "He speaks home, madam; you may relish him more in the soldier than the scholar." Again, precisely! He has put his finger on the truth without knowing how much more there is to Iago – just as she had. Cassio takes Desdemona's hand and provokes one of the most vicious and obscene asides of the play, one surpassed only by jealousy-infected Leontes in *The Winter's Tale*. It is perhaps becoming apparent that the real jealous character in this play is Iago. Cassio's courteous behaviour towards both Emilia and Desdemona has got up his nose. But more is in store, for with Othello's arrival we are obliged to listen (Iago having stimulated the sceptic in us) to some astonishing, dubious and maybe even embarrassing expressions of love, starting with the words "O my fair warrior!":

> It gives me wonder great as my content
> To see you here before me. O, my soul's joy!
> If after every tempest come such calms,
> May the winds blow till they have wakened death,
> And let the labouring bark climb hills of seas,
> Olympus-high, and duck again as low
> As hell's from heaven.

(Act II, scene 1, 177-83)

This is either Shakespeare giving us beautiful poetry (the Othello music) or revealing the character of a truly noble man; it is also plausibly the exposing of someone relying too heavily on absolutes – given to extraordinary poetic flights of fancy about powerful winds, and waves – and exposing an underlying weakness and uncertainty. To Iago they are evidence of bombast circumstance. It makes the audience uneasy; they are aware that fuel is being provided for the accelerating of villainy.

Both Cassio and Othello see love as a form of worship and one effect of this scene, despite Iago's cynicisms, is to idealise Desdemona. Idealising is part of the ennobling game of love. But putting people on a pedestal is, as we all know, dangerous, in that it sets impossible standards. What happens when people don't live up to these? Only Iago, though he acknowledges the possibility in others, when he admits "they say base men being in love have then a nobility in their natures more than is native to them", has no regard for the ennobling power of love: to him it is merely a "permission of the will and a lust of the blood."

What we see is a Desdemona, happy to be "subdued to the very quality" of her lord, nevertheless now trapped in a stereotype. She will conform to this for the rest of the play, even to the point of accepting the blame (though this may also be applauded as an instance of Christian selflessness) for her downfall. The stereotype is confirmed when, in Act IV scene 1, Othello, wavering, describes her as "so delicate with her needle, an admirable musician. O, she will sing the savageness out of a bear! Of so high and plenteous wit and invention!"

The above anticipates feminist criticisms of the play. The woman who defied convention, who spoke out strongly in her defence, becomes the pretty and adoring wife, an adjunct, an extension of her husband's manly honour.

Her husband's utterances on his reunion with her in Cyprus do not help. Both Othello and Desdemona are exposed to the invisible worm flying in the night.

8 Content so Absolute

Love, if we study the comedies, comes in at the eyes as a form of madness, a sickness. It makes people as inconstant as the changing moon when they should be as chaste as the stars and betrays them into folly and distraction; it can, on the other hand, as Helena says in *A Midsummer Night's Dream*, 'transpose to form and dignity.' But for it to do this it has to be tested and brought in line by reason. Othello and Desdemona declare interest in each other's *minds* and, ideally, that is the way it should be. But Othello expresses love for Desdemona in terms that do not compound with sense, sounding more like Orsino in *Twelfth Night* when he claims that his love "is all hungry as the sea/And can digest as much": his languishings reveal a man more in love with the idea of love or wanting to wear it like a fashionable accoutrement. In the comedies lovers are comical because their behaviour and what they say, infected by Cupid's dart, the Moon and fashionable language, expose them to inconstancy. Constancy is the true nature of love. "Love is not love/ Which alters when it alteration findes."

We must be suspicious of those who make unreasonable claims for the quality of love they declare. On their reunion in Cyprus, Othello tells his wife:

> If it were now to die,
> 'Twere now to be most happy; for I fear
> My soul hath her content so absolute
> That not another comfort like to this
> Succeeds in unknown fate.

(Act II, scene 1, 183-187)

This gets from her the shocked response we noted earlier. We ask ourselves: are these romantic sentiments to be treated as the expression of a great love ... a sort of Heathcliff/Catherine love so powerful it can only find its proper satisfaction beyond the grave? In other words a transcendental (if we take the dictionary definition of "beyond the limits of ordinary experience") affair, like that of Antony and Cleopatra? Part of us wants to think so, wants to value the ecstatic, the blissful moment, maybe as a glimpse into something 'realer than real'. If Othello were saying this of the consummation of his marriage (which of course hasn't happened yet) or as the statement of emotional relief, we would be more sympathetic. But this, a reunion after a time at sea, is more a trumpeting to the world (noble as it may sound) not so much of love as it is meant to be but a dependence on the idea of it. He is later to make equally grandiose statements about revenge. If he were a young man in a comedy we would expect amusing consequences to ensue followed by a happy ending. On the quayside at Cyprus after a storm and in the hearing of others, notably Iago, it suggests a serious design fault in the man's character, a fault – though it may also in part be the man's response to the pressures of his situation – which will be exposed again and again and used against him.

9   Motiveless Malignity

We have been too long bemused by this fine alliteration, this description Coleridge has given us of Iago. It has been a godsend to setters of essay titles and exam questions. Motiveless? No, not unless we dismiss the ones he himself gives us as 'mere' fantasy. We have to recognise that to fantasists fantasies are real. Malignity? Yes, but not if we mean some sort of external evil. That's too easy. Iago does not come from an alien world. He is a dramatically created embodiment of characteristics we find in *this* world, the world we know and see around us all the time. I began by suggesting he is the taint in our natures or, to use a Jungian word, our 'shadow', or again, to use the phrase of Blake, one of the two contrary states of the human soul. More down-to-earth, let's suggest there is one in every pub: the chap telling the dirty jokes, ingratiating himself with false bonhomie, and studiously avoiding buying a round. Every time we find ourselves smarmily supporting a cynicism or resenting the good fortune of someone else there is something of Iago about us. The too-easy use of a word like 'evil' is a self-defeating attempt to dissociate ourselves from moral responsibility.

The play's original audience may well have expected something of the anarchic Vice of the old morality plays and something of the Italian, Machiavelli, whom they saw as a master of intrigue, the schoolmaster of slaughter, the filthy poisoner, and whose Christian name, Nicholas, has given us a familiar title for the Devil. To such an audience, Renaissance Italy was like the world reported in our tabloids – wicked and fascinating, happening elsewhere. In Shakespeare's principal source for the play, Giraldo Cinthio's *Hecatommithi,* printed in Italy in the sixteenth century, we learn:

> Now amongst the soldiery there was an Ensign, a man of handsome figure, but of the most depraved nature in the world. This man was in great favour with the Moor, who had not the slightest idea of his wicked- ness; for, despite the malice lurking in his heart, he cloaked with proud and valorous speech and with a specious presence the villainy of his soul that he was to all outward show another Hector or Hercules ... Now the wicked Ensign, regardless of the faith he had pledged his wife,

no less than of friendship, fidelity, and obligation which he owed the Moor, fell passionately in love with Disdemona, and bent all his thoughts to achieve his conquest; yet he dared not to declare his passion openly, fearing that, should the Moor perceive it, he would at once kill him. He therefore sought in various ways, and with secret guile, to betray his passion to the lady; but she, whose every wish was centered on the Moor, had no thought for this Ensign more than for any man; and all the means he tried to gain her love had no more effect than if he had not tried them.

Cinthio's villain is a thwarted seducer whose motivations are simple ones – lust and revenge. But Shakespeare makes something 'real', psychologically very sophisticated of Iago. Acting the part you soon realise the miraculous thing Shakespeare has done in creating a character thinking on his feet, thinking his way through the action of play, attempting to direct its course:

> 'Tis here, but yet confused:
> Knavery's plain face is never seen till used.

> (Act II, scene 1, 302-3)

It is worth noting that in comedies complication is left in the hands of Fate or Time. In *Twelfth Night* Viola says:

> O Time, thou must untangle this, not I;
> It is too hard a knot for me t' untie.

> (Act II, scene 2, 40-1)

In comedies accident and coincidence help shape events. In tragedies events arise more out of character. This is not to ignore the fact that there are moments where the action may tantalisingly take a different course from the one it actually does or we are offered the prospect of alternatives that do not occur. Tragedy plays a serious game with us of 'If only' and 'Yes but' and, ultimately, 'Too late'.

Motivated by hatred, Iago has only a general aim or terminus in mind: the downfall of Othello. He promotes limited action and waits to see what the outcome is before deciding what to do next. But we must, I believe, beware of thinking he has a great and complex mind – whatever intellect he has (let us rather call it wit), it is no scholar's, as Cassio declared to Desdemona, but rather that of a cunning, hard-bitten, small-minded 'man-of-the-world'. It is a barrack-room mentality he possesses. It is not a good idea to bring him on to the stage as someone who looks as though he possesses the experience of a 'mature' middle-aged figure. He is, after all, 28 years old.

Driven by hatred and with a stinging consciousness of having been slighted, he too values his reputation. "I know my price; I am worth no worse a place." He has been passed over in the promotion stakes, after engaging "three great ones of the city/ In personal suit" to speak on his behalf and he doesn't think much of the man who got the job he expected to get. It looks like a case not only of thwarted ambition but also of losing face. This may be considered genuine and motive enough.

He hates and derides Othello's way with language, characterising it as "bombast circumstance,/ Horribly stuffed with epithets of war". As well as having the effect, before we meet Othello, of making us expect an encounter with the stock figure of the braggart soldier, it also provides a contrast to the way we hear Othello speak when we do meet him.

And Iago hates the Florentine Cassio, for his good looks and because he is a theory man:

> That never set a squadron in the field,
> Nor the division of a battle knows

(Act I, scene 1, 22-23)

whereas he himself is an experienced and practical soldier, proud of "my own gained knowledge." In addition, both Othello and Cassio are outsiders, at present valued more highly than he, a native-born Venetian. He even states that Othello has broken the rules of promotion. When we get deeper into the play we may perhaps allow ourselves to ask why Othello actually did choose Cassio for his lieutenant. Were there personal reasons – reward for Cassio's assistance in helping him secure his marriage to Desdemona? If so, doesn't this too add legitimacy to Iago's resentment?

It might be argued that Iago's office of ensign (i.e. the bearer of

Othello's standard) is for him too close a symbolic identification with Othello, someone he purports to hate. Such a discomfort may be further explanation of his resentment. The image of himself as something less than his estimation of his own worth can either be seen as fuelling an arrogance or as the workings of a profound inferiority complex. He hates being held in an inferior position, which he interprets as servility and therefore decides on self-seeking and mischief. Whether this is consequently a newly-created self-image or the bolstering of what he has always been is a real question but it is one we can find no answer to since it leads us into the trap of presupposing a life outside the text. That doesn't mean it is not worth asking. But let's remember we have only what is said in the play and in the complex of contexts it provides.

In stating that:

> Others there are
> Who, trimmed in forms and visages of duty,
> Keep yet their hearts attending on themselves.

> (Act I, scene 1, 49-51)

he is shocking the Elizabethan audience not just by averting them to the fact that here is the villain of the piece but also by articulating their anxiety over different kinds of thinking filtering into the consciousness of the times, the individualism of dangerous free-thinking types who question authority and declare that a human being can carve out his/her own fate – ideas that find some of their articulation in Machiavelli's treatise, *The Prince,* in which it is asserted that the acquisition of power and its use may necessitate methods that are unethical. This was seen as a sinister, subversive kind of pragmatism. Marlowe had created a storm with Tamburlaine's boast:

> I hold the Fates bound fast in iron chains,
> And with my hand turn Fortune's wheel about

> (Act I, scene 2, 174-5 of Part One)

and Faustus':

> Oh, what a world of profit and delight,
> Of power, of honour, of omnipotence,
> Is promised to the studious artisan!
> All things that move between the quiet poles
> Shall be at my command.

> (Act I, scene 1, 52-6)

Marlowe had even brought Machiavelli shockingly on stage in *The Jew of Malta* to scare the audience with these words:

> I count religion but a childish toy,
> And hold there is no sin but ignorance.
> Birds of the air will tell of murders past.
> I am asham'd to hear such fooleries!
> Many will talk of title to a crown:
> What right had Caesar to the empery?
> Might first made kings, and laws were then most sure
> When, like the Draco's, they were writ in blood.

> (Prologue 14-21)

Shakespeare gives us Cassius, whom Julius Caesar rightly sees as dangerous, who says:

> The fault, dear Brutus, lies not in our stars
> But in ourselves, that we are underlings.

> (Act I, scene 2, 140-1)

Edmund, in *King Lear*, is the classic expression:

> This is the excellent foppery of the world, that when we are sick in fortune, often the surfeits of our own behaviour, we make guilty of our disasters the sun, the moon, and stars; as if we were villains on necessity; fools by heavenly compulsion; knaves, thieves, and treachers by spherical predominance; drunkards and liars, and adulterers by an enforced obedience of planetary influence; and all that we are evil in by a divine thrusting on.

> (Act I, scene 2, 128-36)

Iago despises that quality, so dear to many during the Renaissance, of virtue. "Virtue? A fig!" To him, the embodiments of the Good – or rather aspirants towards it – are "an erring barbarian" married to a "supersubtle Venetian". They are fair game. ("Mark me with what violence she first loved the Moor, but for bragging and telling her fantastical lies.") Haven't they set themselves up for it? Isn't there sport to be had?

> The Moor is of a free and open nature,
> That thinks men honest that but seem to be so,
> And will as tenderly be led by th' nose
> As asses are.

(Act I, scene 2, 393-396)

Consider how easily Roderigo can be gulled:

> Thus do I ever make my fool my purse:
> For I mine own gained knowledge should profane
> If I would time expend with such a snipe
> But for my sport and profit.

(Act I, scene 3, 377-390)

Some of the justifications we have listed above are uttered, of course, to persuade Roderigo. They are said for effect. How much validity as motives they have is uncertain. This ambivalence is part of the dramatic experience we undergo in the theatre and argue about on the way home.

It was suggested earlier that soliloquies, even when they seem to be confiding in the audience, do not necessarily deliver the truth. Iago could be said to be gulling the audience into collusion. His first soliloquy coming at the end of Act I piles up further slights to his valuation of himself. People say ("it is thought abroad") that Othello has cuckolded him. "I know not if it be true/ But I for mere suspicion in that kind,/ Will do, as if for surety." He is prepared to believe it in any case in order to feed his mischief. Here is someone caught in a tension between truth and fantasy. I nearly said 'victim of' but that is perhaps running ahead. The secret may well lie in the phrase "for my sport and profit" and the confession that he wishes to "plume up my will" – i.e. to gratify his ego (though "will" too has a sexual meaning). At this point it is worth noting a predilection he has for sexual imagery, engendering and giving birth, as well as his constant references to Hell and night.

In his soliloquy at the end of Act II he repeats the claim that Othello has poisoned his mind (though he describes it in terms of physical pain) by cuckolding him and even proclaims a love (and a lust) for Desdemona. With Cinthio's Ensign we are in no doubt about his lust for the Moor's wife ... but Shakespeare knows how to play the more subtle game of ambivalences.

Is not this man jealous? He even suspects Cassio with his nightcap. Now we start to suspect that here we have a man whose sexual fantasy is highly developed, someone who works "by wit and not by witchcraft" and takes pride in doing so, pride in his own ingenuity in gulling others and exhilaration in the dangerous risk-taking it involves. He sees others through a lens that distorts them to his own shape. Some commentators go as far as to call this a kind of artistry and see in him some kind of portrait of an artist, someone daring to call conventional values into question. In an age of conceptual art, in which art is art simply because its creator declares it to be so and in which irony is valued more highly than straightforwardness, this interpretation is a temptation. It is, as I hope to show, a perverse view.

10 Good Name in Man or Woman

If we are right in saying that Iago experiences (or tenaciously imagines) an insult to his reputation in not getting the promotion he earnestly sought, it is an easy matter to see him, as a consequence of this, as the cynic scorning and vengefully demeaning the reputations of others: Othello is a braggart, Cassio a "bookish theoric", Desdemona a "supersubtle Venetian".

Reputation is a precious ingredient (jewel) of the 'immortal soul'; it is not only the way a character sees him/herself but also how they need to be seen in the eyes of the world – and ultimately the eyes of God. It is a matter of honour to maintain and nourish reputation; loss of it turns you into a beast. There is a long tradition of heroes seeking honour as vital to immortality; it is the record you leave behind you that matters. Heroes all wish a true account of themselves preserved, to reach into posterity.

In this play there are those to whom the word 'free' is constantly applied; it suggests openness and honesty, a generous nature, loyalty and a willingness to give credit where credit is due; it implies modesty and, especially in the case of a Cassio, good manners. Iago has a reputation for honesty to maintain, kept up as artifice, a mask: for most of the play only Roderigo and the audience know of his cynicism and hypocrisy.

To see oneself aright requires a proper self-love (as the Dauphin reminds us in *Henry V* "Self-love ... is not so vile a sin/ As self-neglecting"); to be judged virtuous in the eyes of the world and ultimately God, requires virtuous behaviour, to be on the side of the angels. When we first meet Othello we are impressed; this is not the man we have been led to expect: here, we feel, is someone in control of himself and protective of his reputation; his language is noble, self-possessed; he resists Iago's suggestion that he should be politic and avoid the wrath of Brabantio ("You were best go in"), rejecting it as dishonourable:

Not I. I must be found.
My parts, my title, and my perfect soul
Shall manifest me rightly.

(Act I, scene 2, 30-32)

He will not be seen acting in a cowardly manner:

For know, Iago,
But that I love the gentle Desdemona,
I would not my unhousèd free condition
Put into circumscription and confine
For the seas' worth.

(Act I, scene 2, 24-28)

The word 'gentle' will continue to be applied to Desdemona; and here too is the image of the sea's vastness he likes so much.

We, nowadays, hear the word 'gentle' emotionally, with the meaning 'pleasant' and 'kind' (as in being kind to animals) but in the hierarchically-structured world of the Elizabethans and Jacobeans its primary meaning is 'well-born; belonging to a family of position'; its opposite would be a word like 'base' or, more significantly, 'unnatural'. And while we are talking of antonyms, let me suggest (and this ties in with the tensions between opposites discussed earlier) that Shakespeare's audience, because of the interconnectedness of their universe (now beginning to look as though it might fall apart) was accustomed to thinking analogically and with an implicit awareness of opposites. The syllogism lies at the heart of such thinking.

Othello's sentiments are noble but Shakespeare is also programming us with indications that there is a perilous dependence on absolutes.

The first time the Moor is mentioned by actual name is in Act I, scene 3 where the Duke qualifies it with the word "valiant". Before this we have heard of a "lascivious Moor", "the thick-lips", "an old black ram", "a Barbary horse" and, significantly – given the play's insistence on mentioning the denizens and properties of Hell – a devil who will make a grandsire of Brabantio.

His soldierly qualities are urgently needed "Against the general enemy Ottoman". But state business is peremptorily interrupted by Brabantio with a speech that is both an echo of Othello's 'seas' worth' and a pre-echo of his later utterances, when he declares:

> ... my particular grief
> Is of so flood-gate and o'erbearing nature
> That it engluts and swallows other sorrows,
> And yet is still itself.

(Act I, scene 3, 55-8)

Is this vehement language rhetoric or the expression of a genuine grief?

Desdemona insists she:

> ... saw Othello's visage in his mind
> And to his honours and his valiant parts
> Did I my soul and fortunes consecrate.

(Act I, scene 3, 249-251)

The religious vocabulary is significant. She sees the relationship as a matter of the souls, as an act of consecration lacking only in its proper rite of consummation. If she is not allowed to travel to Cyprus "The rites for why I love him are bereft me".

It is at this point Othello is quick to point out that he is not driven by inordinate sexual desire. The play asks whether self-image and reputation are always the same thing.

To Shakespeare's Christian audience, temptation was familiar as the work of the Devil and he and his agents operated in the real world. Hamlet has to test the ghost of his father because chance was it might be the devil come to grab his soul. The history of the world began with the temptations of Adam and Eve resulting in the Original Sin ("Man's first disobedience, and the fruit/Of that forbidden tree, whose mortal taste/ Brought death into the world, and all our woe,/ With loss of Eden"); and of course there was the Devil vainly tempting Christ in the wilderness. The Devil was no fable but a force at work in people's daily lives, determined to undermine and destroy God's creation.

Cassio we know is a proper man and in Iago's plot to bring him down and use this event to bring Othello down, we see him as virtuous, resisting, and by degrees yielding, to temptation. Iago obliges him (a man with "very poor and unhappy brains for drinking") to join in a bawdy roistering drunken sing-song. Always loyal, Cassio, after an initial reluctance to give into a self-confessed weakness, drinks to "our general" and, when asked whether he wants to hear the salacious ditty about King Stephen's britches again, declares "No, for I hold him to be unworthy of his place that does those things." This is again an expression of loyalty and a confirmation that the virtuous man knows his duty and his place. It is a matter of honour and good name. When Cassio is disgraced the others involved (though they have previously talked of informing on him) and in particular Iago, pretend it is a matter of honour not to betray him publicly, though Iago is clever enough to say:

> I had rather have this tongue cut from my mouth
> Than it should do offence to Michael Cassio.

> (Act 2, scene 3, 215-6)

This is interpreted by Othello as "honesty and love" mincing the matter and making it "light to Cassio". Honesty is the proper face of honour. Cassio later exclaims to Iago:

> Reputation, reputation, reputation! O, I have lost my reputation! I have lost the immortal part of myself, and what remains is bestial.

> (Act 2, scene 3, 255-7)

The equation is: reputation is an aspect of the soul; loss of it reduces a man to the level of the beast. We may indeed sympathise with Cassio's predicament (even if he has brought it upon himself by yielding to temptation) but we may also remember – with a sneaking sympathy – Falstaff's tirade against honour and reputation. Notice how in this scene drunkenness and wrath are called devils.

After the brawl and the wounding of Montano, it is difficult for Cassio to climb back into favour. He has after all hurt someone "of great fame in Cyprus and great affinity". In other words he has affected the honour of someone else. This tells us that honour is not just an individual but a family matter: it is a betraying of the blood. One of the many meanings attached to the word 'blood' includes, as already stated, a genetic one, that of breeding and therefore social standing.

Whereas Cassio is open to Iago's persuasions to take steps to regain favour and rebuild his reputation, Othello is not:

> ... to be once in doubt
> Is once to be resolved.

> (Act III, scene 3, 177-8)

Now we remember "when I love thee not,/Chaos is come again" and the speech in which he equates disgrace with the loss of all his military honour:

> Farewell the tranquil mind! Farewell content!
> Farewell the plumèd troops and the big wars
> That make ambition virtue – O, farewell!
> Farewell the neighing steed, and the shrill trump,
> The spirit-stirring drum, th' ear-piercing fife,
> The royal banner and all quality,
> Pride, pomp and circumstance of glorious war!
> And, O you mortal engines, whose rude throats
> Th' immortal Jove's dread clamours counterfeit,
> Farewell! Othello's occupation's gone.

> (Act III, scene 3, 345-54)

We either see this as the despair of a man who has known nothing but warfare all his life, and as expressing an orthodox attitude to war as 'glorious' and one of the most potent means of accruing honour (Iago values "action glorious"), or as the bombast circumstances Iago described at the beginning of the play. Or is Shakespeare simply writing great poetic speeches for his leading actor, Richard Burbage? The answer is a dynamic mixture of all of them.

The central statement concerning reputation and honour is of course, ironically, that of Iago:

Good name in man or woman, dear my lord,
Is the immediate jewel of their souls
Who steals my purse, steals trash; 'tis something, nothing;
'Tis mine, 'tis his, and has been slave to thousands:
But he that filches from me my good name
Robs me of that which not enriches him
And makes me poor indeed.

(Act III, scene 3, 154-60)

The words are uttered as a kind of blunt wisdom, to the point of sounding platitudinous. In the emotional context of the scene they are part of a disingenuous beating about the bush, a form of verbal torture that exploits uncertainty and has Othello exclaim: "By heaven, I'll know thy thoughts."

Honour of course has a sexual dimension. The expression 'a woman's honour', even if it may sound old-fashioned to some ears, still has some currency. It means chastity or purity; and a reverence for chastity is a determining aspect of Shakespeare's plays. We remember Prospero's instructions to Ferdinand:

Then, as my gift, and thine own acquisition
Worthily purchased, take my daughter. But
If thou dost break her virgin-knot before
All sanctimonious ceremonies may
With full and holy rite be minist'red,
No sweet aspersion shall the hevens let fall
To make thy contract grow; but barren hate,
Sour-eyed disdain, and discord shall bestrew
The union of they bed with weeds so loathly
That you shall hate it both. Therefore take heed,
As Hymen's lamps shall light you.

(*The Tempest*, Act IV, scene 1, 14-23)

In other words, sex is only permissible (sanctified) in marriage. Similar injunctions are laid upon Perdita and Florizel in *A Winter's Tale;* and *Measure for Measure* cannot operate without our understanding the critical importance of chastity. Chastity operates within marriage through constancy, fidelity to one's partner for life.

50

11   The Green-eyed Monster

It was Lily B. Campbell who taught us to understand jealousy in the way the Elizabethans did, as a "derivative or compound passion". Envy was seen as a species of hatred; hatred was the obverse of love. Campbell quotes from *The French Academie* of 1594 in which the author writes "I understand by jealousy, a feare which a man hath, lest another whome he would not, should enjoy something". Envy/jealousy stimulates anger ("the devil wrath") and desire for revenge. The Devil was known as the "Envious Man, that soweth tares amongst the wheat by night". So there is a defined connection between jealousy, fear, hatred and evil. There is also obviously the desire to mar or destroy something belonging to someone else. We have pointed out that the keynote of hatred is sounded three times within the first seven lines of the play. When Iago's poison has entered Othello's soul he exclaims "I am abused, and must loathe her". We witness Iago making dedications to evil on two occasions. Envy, of course, is one of the Seven Deadly Sins familiar to audiences of morality plays and seen on stage in Marlowe's *Doctor Faustus* (written around 1588) where it is given the words:

> I am envy, begotten of a chimney-sweeper and an oyster-wife. I cannot read and therefore wish all books were burnt. I am lean with seeing others eat. Oh, that there would come a famine over all the world, that all might die, and I live alone, then thou should'st see how fat I'd be. But must thou sit and I stand? Come down with a vengeance!

> (Act II, scene 1, 132-8)

Emilia tells us that jealousy is "begot upon itself, born on itself". And this is perhaps the reason Coleridge talked of "the motive-hunting of motiveless malignity" as if Iago is simply making it all up, merely fantasising. This is, naturally, partly true. He suspects the lusty Moor:

> Hath leaped into my seat, the thought whereof
> Doth, like a poisonous mineral, gnaw my inwards.

> (Act II, scene 1, 287-8)

He thinks the same of Cassio and we wonder what evidence he has. Are we to imagine these events as the perks of soldiers? Do we expect Othello at the time of his marriage to be as much a virgin as he and society expect Desdemona to be? We can't expect answers because they lie outside the text – but this, again, doesn't necessarily mean it is invalid to ask them.

Like all psychopaths, Iago is a *seeming*-rational man taking pride in the fact that he works "by wit and not by witchcraft"; he doesn't fully understand he is rationalising a fantasy. Like Edmund's in *King Lear*, his view of the world is the cynic's caricature, the fantasy world of an embittered and frustrated satirist. ("I confess it is my nature's plague/ To spy into abuses, and of my jealousy/ Shape faults that are not.") Iago cannot separate caricature from reality. There is no place for love or virtue in his world. His language tells us that here is someone whose sexual fantasy is highly charged and obscene. He is jealous of his wife, sees Othello and Cassio as sexual predators; imagines himself in love with Desdemona and admits to lusting after her; his sick mind can even gain pleasure from imagining her degraded by Roderigo. He enjoys thinking of sexual encounters between Desdemona and Othello. Cassio talks of the consummation of their marriage as a kind of benison when in Cyprus he wishes:

> That he may bless this bay with his tall ship,
> Make love's quick pants in Desdemona's arms,
> Give renewed fire to our extinct spirits.

> (Act II, scene 1, 79-81)

What Iago tells Roderigo reveals an entirely different mentality at work:

> Her eye must be fed. And what delight shall she have to look on the devil? When the blood is made dull with the act of sport, there should be, again to inflame it and give satiety a fresh appetite, loveliness in favour, sympathy in years, manners and beauties: all which the Moor is defective in.

> (Act II, scene 1, 219-24)

If, in performance, such words are given a certain relish – as I'm sure they should – then we have a man who lives vicariously and gets a thrill from doing so. Life is a sport, sex is a sport: his plots are deliberately engineered for self-gratification ("to plume up my will").

What we are saying here is that the most jealous man in this play is Iago, one who clearly knows that:

> Trifles light as air
> Are to the jealous confirmations strong
> As proofs of holy writ.

(Act III, scene 3, 319-21)

It takes one to know one. And on that note it is worth remarking that we have only to read the Sonnets to know that Shakespeare himself was intimate with the power of jealousy. Take Sonnet 57, for example, where we find:

> Being your slave what should I do but tend,
> Upon the houres, and times of your desire?
> I have no precious time at al to spend;
> No services to do til you require.
> Nor dare I chide the world without end houre,
> Whilst I (my soveraine) watch the clock for you,
> Nor thinke the bitternesse of absence sowre,
> When you have bid your servant once adieu.
> Nor dare I question with my jealous thought,
> Where you may be, or your affaires suppose,
> But like a sad slave stay and thinke of nought
> Save where you are, how happy you make those.
>   So true a foole is love, that in your Will,
>   (Though you doe any thing) he thinkes no ill.

12 By Wit, and not by Witchcraft

There are those who see Iago's abilities as the workings of genius. Harold Bloom, for instance, considers him a great artist, whose villainy is "heroic", who possesses a "negative grace" – an artist highly skilled in the "arts of disinformation, disorientation, and derangement", who evinces "the perfections of malign will and genius for hatred." This is to let the sneaking admiration we feel for him during the play exist beyond the play's proper outcome, in which "heroic villainy" is seen for what it is: opposed to any aspiration towards that which is considered good, honourable and virtuous. Better to see Iago the way Hazlitt does (quoted by Bloom), as the embodiment of a "diseased mental activity", as someone who "stabs men in the dark to prevent *ennui*".

Acting the part, you might be persuaded that he is a consummate actor, a shrewd manipulator, a highly-skilled puppet-master. His skill – if this is not too complimentary a word – lies in his ability to isolate others so that they become victims of their own ignorance, innocence, weakness. Notice how he eggs Roderigo on in the first scene to create mayhem, then, stepping into the shadow, shouts loudest and the most obscenely from its comparative safety and anonymity. Then, having caused the chaos, he disappears, like the politic creature he is, to be with Othello offering a fine pretence of loyalty and concern. We have noticed how he tries unsuccessfully to persuade the Moor to "best go in" out of the way of Brabantio's grief and anger. (What would have been the result if Othello had taken this advice?)

Iago is not a genius but a vulgar opportunist and gambler.

There are many instances of this ability of his to isolate his victims: he gets the disgraced Cassio aside to manipulate him; likewise he engineers private moments to poison Othello's ear; isolates him so that he overhears Cassio's slighting of Bianca, and so on. This isolating of people is another aspect of the claustrophobic effects at work in the play, which we noted earlier on. And let's not forget the fact that Othello is already isolated (visibly) by virtue of the colour of his skin and to some extent by his elopement-marriage and his age.

Iago has gulled Roderigo into making him believe he will act as a go-between in the former's suit to Desdemona. The practical absurdity of this never occurs to Roderigo – as of course, more crucially, the absurdity in practical terms of an affair between Desdemona and Cassio never occurs to Othello. We learn from Brabantio that Roderigo's attentions have been unwelcome but that doesn't deter him either. It is not because he possesses an obstinacy, a strong will to persist, but more a stupidity and a pliant ear – and because also he is in thrall to and blinded by lust. This is food to Iago's fantasy. How much credence we give to Iago's financially exploiting Roderigo ("Thus do I ever make my fool my purse") is another matter. It feels more of a secondary concern, a bonus. Thus Shakespeare is perhaps signalling more villainy than necessary. Several times in the play Roderigo realises his case is hopeless but is then easily persuaded that Iago has his interests at heart. Roderigo is pushed into adopting the same cynicism and language, as eventually is Othello, and forced to believe that things are not what they seem.

If we acknowledge an interweaving of echo, pre-echo and parody in the play then the gulling of Roderigo becomes, with hindsight, a parody of the undermining of Othello.

It is not without irony that Iago claims to use wit, since wit, in its meaning of mind/reason/understanding/judgement/intelligence, is an angelic quality. Wit to us has come to stand for a tricksy kind of humour. Our tendency is to pluralise it so as to mean cleverness/ ingenuity/intrigue. But that way we miss out on the fearful irony of witnessing a white man, the blackest of devils, boasting of an attribute of the angelic orders. Part of us wants to admire this, as Marlowe admired the vauntings of Tamburlaine and the ambitions of Faustus.

Though he often talks of poisons – ("The Moor already changes with my poison") and is in the audience's eyes another projection of those terrifying Italian poisoners, whose stories they enjoyed seeing on the stage or reading about in books like Nashe's *The Unfortunate Traveller* (1594), Iago doesn't of course deal in actual poisons (as does, say, Hamlet's Uncle); he doesn't use charms or drugs (as Othello is accused of using). His poisons are verbal ones – from the casual remark (that isn't at all casual) to subtle innuendo to downright lie:

> Dangerous conceits are in their natures poisons,
> Which at the first are scarce found to distaste,

But, with a little, act upon the blood,
Burn like the mines of sulphur.

(Act III, scene 3, 323-6)

And when Othello at this point makes an appearance we hear him saying:

Not poppy, nor mandragora,
Nor all the drowsy syrups of the world,
Shall ever medicine thee to that sweet sleep
Which thou owed'st yesterday.

(Act III, scene 3, 327-30)

Like Othello at the start of the play, Iago attempts to be a controller of language: he is also, as Feste jokingly claims in *Twelfth Night*, a "corrupter of words". Othello uses language to create a self-image rooted in nobility; Iago uses language to undermine and destroy. He triumphs when Othello finally adopts his way of talking. This is another feature of what we've called the play's 'logic'.

Of course Iago's main skill is in insinuating doubt and, luckily, his main quarry is a man for whom to be in doubt is once to be resolved. I say luckily because, whatever skill Iago may take pride in, he still has to rely on luck – to hope that, if he can't make his own luck, it will nonetheless favour him. The opportunist, the gambler, needs to at least put himself in the way of possible success. It is this playing with luck that is the heart of all sport. Comedies leave things to Fate and Chance, relying heavily on coincidence and mistaken identities being marvellously revealed. In tragedies, characters, believing in free-will, try to make their luck or make luck work for them. And yet it is part of the dynamics of tragedy to suggest to us too that, in the words of Kent in *King Lear*, "It is the stars,/ The stars above us, govern our conditions." Or Gloucester in the same play saying "As flies to wanton boys, are we to th' gods,/ They kill us for their sport." This too then is part of the grip tragedy has on us: this ambivalence that either sees man exercising free-will and making choices or as a fatal victim of forces beyond his control – in other words that what is willed is merely a baffling aspect of a greater will and pre-ordained. But men resent and resist this view. It is part of the ambivalence that fires the creative energies of the play.

Part of Iago's skill is – something we admire in comedians – his sense of timing. There is also his ability to seize the moment and improvise. Emilia 'comes across' the handkerchief and hands it over to him; Bianca turns up at opportune/inopportune moments. Iago often has to think on his feet. Part of an audience's reaction is to wonder how long his luck will hold or, rather, knowing it *must* eventually run out, at what point it is going to do so. There are times he has to think quickly, for example in Act IV he needs to plot to kill Cassio, now named Governor of Cyprus, if he is to avoid Othello returning to Venice before his plot may or may not come to fruition.

As well as needing luck on its side, wit has its limitations, to ignore which is a form of blind arrogance – to use Aristotle's word, *hubris*. It is *hubris* that brings men down. In Christian terminology the equivalent to *hubris* is the Sin of Pride or Presumption – the assuming of godlike powers (as with those over-reachers Tamburlaine, Faustus and, most obviously, Satan). Pride predicates a fall – as it did the Fall. Wit is based on knowledge and it was Adam and Eve's eating the forbidden fruit of the Tree of Knowledge which brought death, sin and penance into the world. Knowledge brings with it not just death but consciousness of death. It is Iago who brings death with him – not death as legitimised by "glorious war" – but murder.

13   And Talking of Aristotle

Aristotle's *The Poetics* written in the fourth century BC was an attempt to describe the characteristics of Sophocles, *Oedipus Rex*. Its influence or, rather, that of later commentators, who made it seem prescriptive rather than seeing it as descriptive, has been enormous. We have inherited the view that tragedy must be about heroes, about characters 'better' than the majority; that these heroes are subjected to a fall; that they are in some degree responsible for this fall because of a flaw in their natures or an error of judgement (*harmartia*); there is, after much suffering and struggle, a moment of recognition (*peripeteia*) or discovery of the truth, a point of no return; and then a change from ignorance to knowledge (*anagnorisis*) which ironically comes too late to be of any use to the tragic hero. The effect on the audience of witnessing all this, Aristotle called *catharsis* – which hotly-debated term we will ignore, except perhaps to say that it is an attempt to understand that intensity of feeling we experience in watching tragedies and carry away with us afterwards.

It is *harmartia* I wish to draw attention to in particular, mainly because (in the same way that labelling Iago as evil does) it offers too simple, too neat a solution. Hamlet's procrastinations are the key to his play; Lear's lack of self-knowledge compounded by dotage explains him; Macbeth's 'vaulting ambition' is the answer to his predicament; and, of course, Othello can be 'explained' by his jealousy. Thankfully the notion of the 'tragic flaw' has – though it sometimes lingers on in student essays – been ditched. Rather than seeking answers – especially easy ones – we should be thinking of the proper questions we should be asking. The right questions in the study of literature are more important than any 'right' answers.

Does Othello suffer from *hubris*? This is something we will come to later. But let's pose these questions in the meantime: if we make a distinction between ignorance and innocence, to what degree is he therefore culpable? What was the rose in Blake's poem guilty of? What is the relationship between Innocence and Experience? Are they interrelated, parts of a whole?

Othello is Aristotelian only in the sense that it focuses on a relatively small number of characters and concentrates intensely and almost exclusively on a linear plot.

14 Saints in your Injuries, Devils being Offended

In Act II, scene 1, Emilia is projected cynically by her husband as the traditional scold, a long-standing onstage tradition going back in England to the mystery plays and Noah's wife. She answers his cynicisms by telling him "You have little cause to say so" and "You shall not write my praise" ("praise" meaning eulogy or epitaph). To what extent does this provocative mockery – meant as a kind of diversion while waiting for Othello to land in Cyprus – represent Iago's real feelings about women? Does his opinion of Cassio as a "fellow almost damned in a fair wife" offer a clue? That he sees marriage as a form of damnation? If one of his talents is invention then this performance at the quayside is strangely underpowered and lacks the comic zest to make it really entertaining and pointedly meaningful in the manner we expect of Shakespeare clowns. Is he underplaying it here in a parody of courtesy, *knowing* it to be banal? This certainly seems to be the effect of the platitudinous rhyming couplets he offers – a kind of pseudo-wit. Or is it a glimpse into man as he 'really is'? As we have noted earlier, Desdemona, without quite realising it, sees this banality for what it is – that she does so is an irony for us to relish. Cassio, in a confirmation of her innocence, excuses him with "He speaks home, madam. You may relish him more in the soldier than the scholar".

We know that Iago is 28 years old and so may surmise that his wife is a similar age. Having to work for a living, she is more a woman of the world than Desdemona, more practical; and she is, of course, the key to the play's dénouement – another of its ironies. It is she who first sees through and, defying obedience, uncovers her husband's machinations.

In Act IV, scene 3 she acts as a sounding board for her mistress's thoughts and their accompanying undercurrent of anxiety. The ironic parallel of this with the 'seduction' scenes between Iago and Othello hardly needs pointing out.

The play asks us very simply to what extent do wives understand husbands and husbands wives, and tells us that marriage, to work properly, has to rely on trust and (here's a word!) honesty. Vows of chastity and fidelity, though made before God, are nothing without honesty. It is honesty that makes the world go round.

We know that Othello and Desdemona have not been married long enough (mere days) for the marriage to be more a matter of hope than achievement. They really do not know each other, despite their protestations. A question is: how well do Iago and Emilia know each other? We have to acknowledge the fact that wives are required to be obedient if we are to understand Emilia's handing over of the handkerchief and her belated exposure of her husband and his involvement in and responsibility for the 'tragic loading' of the bed. It is then that a 'higher' form of obedience, an obedience to truth is demanded.

Emilia is a faithful servant of her mistress, trusted to the point of outspokenness:

> Emilia   Dismiss me?
>
> Desdemona   It was his bidding: therefore, good Emilia,
>   Give me my nightly wearing, and adieu.
>   We must not now displease him.
>
> Emilia   I would you had never seen him!
>
> (Act IV, scene 3, 13-17)

She attends her mistress faithfully and sometimes chides her in a motherly fashion. She also knows that there are times when it is kinder simply to chatter.

In an ironic parallel to the scene at the quayside, Desdemona catechises her:

> Dost thou in conscience – think tell me, Emilia –
> That there be women do abuse their husbands
> In such gross kind?
>
> (Act IV, scene 3, 58-60)

The reply, though teasing, is given in a gentle manner. It may be said to be a better example of the use of wit than her husband's. She gives us a defence of wives that suggests not just knowledge and observation but experience. She is aware of the faults of husbands, blaming them "If their wives do fall". And she includes the possibility of physical violence in husbands' behaviour towards their wives (though we can't know, we can still ask if she has been a victim of this) when she says "or say they strike us" – something which we have shockingly witnessed two scenes earlier when Othello, in front of Lodovico, the newly-arrived representative of Venice, strikes Desdemona causing him to say in amazement:

> Is this the noble Moor, whom our full senate
> Call all – in all – sufficient? Is this the nature
> Whom passion could not shake? Whose solid virtue
> The shot of accident nor dart of chance
> Could neither graze nor pierce?

> (Act IV, scene 1, 266-70)

He wonders "did the letters work upon his blood"; and finally makes the judgement in which we all must concur: "I am sorry that I am deceived in him".

In Desdemona's bedroom, Emilia gives a picture of the world of which Desdemona has scant knowledge, having been protected from it as the daughter of a high-ranking Venetian. Again, the question has to be posed: where do we draw the line between ignorance and innocence? Emilia is also outspoken about women's sexual needs:

> And have not we affections,
> Desires for sport, and frailty, as men have?
> Then let them use us well: else let them know,
> The ills we do, their ills instruct us so.

> (Act IV, scene 3, 99-102)

Some of this is for the audience: for the men to jeer at and the women cheer. But it also underscores Desdemona's lack of knowledge of the world, causing her to say:

> Good night, good night. Godme such uses send,
> Not to pick bad from bad, but by bad mend!

> (Act IV, scene 3, 103-4)

In terms of the echoes and pre-echoes we have talked about earlier, we should pick up on words like 'sport', remembering Iago's use of it, and 'use', with both its sense of behave well towards and use sexually.

Emilia is prepared to defend her mistress with her soul. She tells Othello:

> I durst, my lord, to wager she is honest,
> Lay down my soul at stake.

> (Act IV, scene 2, 11-2)

This is put to the test when in the last Act she confronts Othello with the words:

> I care not for thy sword – I'll make thee known,
> Though I lost twenty lives.

> (Act V, scene 2, 164-5

She is prepared to confront her husband too: "Disprove this villain" (meaning Othello), "if thou be'st a man". This last clause "if thou be'st a man" is a challenge that goes straight to the heart of this play's concerns – the difference between what a man is and what he should be and what is meant by manliness.

If we were asked to say who is the most faithful character in the play we would have to say, without any doubt, Emilia. Desdemona, though faithful onto death, may be said to give in to her fate, collude in her own death. Emilia has a courage her mistress, despite being on several occasions called 'warrior', knows nothing about. She dies in the service of truth.

15   A Proper Man and a Notable Strumpet

Cassio is not a particularly complex character. An ostensibly good man, he has two weaknesses, which he tries to keep under control. He cannot take his ale and he consorts with a common courtesan. Both of these are used to undo him. Both expose him to his bestial nature, as he understands well enough when he talks of being "now a sensible man, by and by a fool, and presently a beast".

The word "proper", of course, is Iago's, used sarcastically to suggest someone we are meant to look up to but who is really a man of surfaces, with little or no experience of "glorious war" and not long out of college. It also suggests delicate manners and exemplary behaviour. Iago's line describing him as a "fellow almost damned in a fair wife" implies he's had a fortunate escape from matrimony – either that or it's information (not found in Cinthio) that Shakespeare in the course of writing forgot he'd included. The former at least allows for a parallel with Othello/Desdemona to be drawn.

A young man with a touch of callowness to him, he knows the art of complimenting, has learnt the language of love, doubtless from Petrarch, and courtly manners from Castiglione's *Il Cortegiano* (The Book of the Courtier, 1528, translated into English by 1556). A touch effusive but justifying this in terms of breeding and good manners. Loyal to his master but fatally concealing weaknesses from him.

Again, someone caught between ignorance and innocence. A man on the side of goodness and virtue but, once undermined, confirmed as a fallen creature, tortured in the space betwixt this world and that of grace.

Bianca is, like Othello and Cassio, an outsider. She is a moral outsider; her appearances suggest intrusions of a demi-monde inhabited by women of dubious reputation into polite society. She intrudes into the rhythm of the play but also interferes in an unseemly fashion in the world of men. Her appearances cast a shadow on the character of Cassio. Once we know of her, he is no longer quite the proper man. What does it say of him that he idealises Desdemona yet consorts with Bianca? In some respects, she reminds us of many men's crude need to divide women into virgins and whores – a division that is revealed in Othello too: he idealises Desdemona then castigates her as a whore. Again, we are aware of man's double nature. Hypocrisy if you like. Men should be what they seem. And what does it say about legitimising 'appetites'? – that in a world which prioritises masculine values women are treated as adjuncts to men and must be severely punished when they don't live up to expectations. In the light of this, Emilia's criticism of the behaviour of husbands sounds dangerously radical and 'modern'. Her own crucial intrusion into the world of men, when she exposes her husband's guilt, may be taken as more than seemly or timely: it is as an act of real courage.

Bianca is listed in the dramatis personae as a courtesan, in itself an ambiguous term meaning either one attached to the court of a nobleman or a court-mistress and therefore, euphemistically, a prostitute. Is Bianca what we now call a high-class prostitute? Does it make her any better or worse than a low-class one?

She makes three brief but crucial appearances and each time is, ironically, an innocent pawn in the action. In the first scene in which we meet her (Act III, scene 4) Cassio calls her "fair Bianca" and "sweet love"; in the second (Act IV, scene 1) he likens her slightingly to a perfumed polecat and as someone "haunting" him; in Act V, scene 1 she is called "strumpet" by both Iago and Emilia.

It is obvious that if Cassio is a client he is a favourite one. She is inordinately fond of him. This may be counted as a weakness, for it is this fondness (can we say she is in love with him?) that leads her into trouble beyond any deserving on her part.

And we must not miss the irony of her name, an Italian name that translates as 'white'. The play relies heavily on our constant awareness of the contrast between black and white and an intimate knowledge that black is the colour of all things negative and white the colour of positive things. The play also, it must be said, challenges this symbolism by saying 'Look, here is a black man aspiring towards the Good being destroyed by a white man whose soul is black with sin'. Bianca is morally neither black nor white but the in-between shade of grey.

And of course she underscores the theme of jealousy, when, complaining of Cassio's neglecting her and given Desdemona's handkerchief, she reacts with the words:

This is some token from a newer friend.
To the felt absence now I feel a cause.

(Act III, scene 4, 177-8)

(The word "cause" here is what we mean by pre-echo, adumbrating Othello's more famous use of it).

Cassio's rebuke is interesting. He tells her:

Go to, woman!
Throw your vile guesses in the devil's teeth
From whence you have them. You are jealous now
That this is from some mistress, some remembrance:
No, by my faith, Bianca.

(Act III, scene 4, 179-83)

How different things would have been if Othello had reacted to Iago's insinuations in this fashion!

Cassio likes the handkerchief enough to have it copied and tells Bianca that he wants it done before its owner (he is ignorant of who it belongs to) misses it and wants it back. Here once more is an irony for us to relish. As we have said, there are moments in the play where things might have gone differently and here we have two of them: Othello *could have* told Iago to throw his "vile guesses in the devil's teeth"; the handkerchief *could have* been returned to its owner in good time.

Cassio's excuses for not visiting Bianca for a whole week are simply that he has "this while with leaden thoughts been pressed". He hopes to get back to normal soon. She tells him she will be patient: "I must be circumstanced" – i.e. accept things as they are.

Her next appearance is fatal: she is still jealous and Cassio is less patient with her and she with him. "This is some minx's token" she claims and "If you'll come to supper tonight, you may; if you will not, come when you are next prepared for". I said fatal because all this is overheard by Othello tricked into thinking he now has the "ocular proof" he has demanded.

When the crunch comes for Cassio (when he's wounded and Roderigo is killed at the beginning of Act V) Bianca reaffirms her feelings for him using the words "dear" and "sweet". But this time she has to confront Iago, who, with typical quick-thinking, drags her into his plot:

> Gentlemen all, I do suspect this trash
> To be a party in this injury

(Act V, scene 1, 85-6)

and again:

> Look you pale, mistress?
> Do you perceive the gastness of her eye?
> Nay, if you stare, we shall hear more anon.
> Behold her well; I pray you look upon her.
> Do you see, gentleman? Nay, guiltiness will speak
> Though tongues were out of use.

(Act V, scene 1, 105-110)

The tone of these utterances suggests Iago is just holding back a fearful excitement, near panic. He admits as much in the soliloquising last two lines of the scene:

> This is the night
> That either makes me, or fordoes me quite.

(Act V, scene 1, 128-9)

And so Bianca is arrested, protesting she is no strumpet. And this is the last we hear of her. Again, the question of to what degree she is culpable and deserving of whatever becomes her fate, is left unanswered.

She brings into the play a third kind of woman – one who uses men. The irony is that it would seem that she has fallen for one of her clients. In this light she may be seen as woman as nuisance. It is this that causes her to 'intrude' into the action and become – again ironically – an innocent pawn in it and another of its victims.

16   Mingling Breaths

Like *Macbeth*, but in a different way, *Othello* is sexually charged. In *Macbeth*, Lady Macbeth seeks to control the situation and her husband by using sexual blackmail; in *Othello* it is a palpable part of the dynamic tension of the whole play, in which love is constantly being opposed by lust. A major strand of imagery is drawn from sexually-vigorous animals: goats, asses, monkeys, toads – toads that "knot and gender".

Couplings are significant: there is much kissing. Jonathan Bate has pointed out that "The repeated kiss is a dramatic motif which serves as an iconic representation of Othello's love for Desdemona"; he goes on to remark "The kiss is imagined as a kind of music, Iago as a destroyer of harmony". The taking and holding of hands is equally important. In the cynical eyes of Iago, hands become "sweating devils", which, in keeping with the properties of the humour, blood, become "hot and moist". The sexual innuendoes are obvious, especially when thought of in terms of the carnal appetites of beasts (thought to live only through their senses) – and by implication of human beings when they behave like beasts, when they are "hot as monkeys" or "making the beast with two backs". There is also "mingling of breaths" – again, tying in with the properties of the element, air, that dominates the play. We have already noted allusions to unpleasant smells and to slime.

Kissing and touching hands are observed publicly on the quayside at Cyprus. As with other aspects of the play – notably its language – we are always conscious of surface innocence with an undercurrent of vicious denial. The courtly behaviour of Cassio and Othello's kissing of Desdemona are laid bare to misinterpretation and distortion.

To state the obvious, the play is about a honeymoon. Desdemona insists on going to the wars with her husband because, if she stays in Venice, "The rites for why I love him are bereft me".

He has already stated that he wants her to accompany him:

>   not
> To please the palate of my appetite,
> Nor to comply with heat – the young affects

In me defunct – and proper satisfaction;

(Act I, scene 3, 258-61)

Both of them underestimate the power of the blood.

The relationship between Cassio and Bianca is to all intents and purposes a sexual one in which sex is understood to be a disposable commodity. In such a relationship men's reputations are less precarious, less open to vilification than women's. The relationship is, as we have noted, complicated by the fact that Bianca has fallen for Cassio.

Iago and Emilia both call Bianca a strumpet. Their own relationship can only be a matter of speculation. We can surmise from Iago's cynical attitudes to women that the marriage is at best one of tolerance. When his wife tells him she has the handkerchief with the words "I have a thing for you" he replies "You have a thing for me? It is a common thing" – and the phrase is to be taken as obscene. To him women are "Players in your housewifery, and housewives in your beds"; their only purpose in life is to "suckle fools and chronicle small beer" – which is to say; to people the world with fools and manage household accounts. We have to assume that the marriage is based upon obedience of wife to husband – that is until she finds a courage to expose him as a villain. Her attitudes to men, as expressed to Desdemona in Act IV, scene 3, suggest long-suffering (they are not too far removed from her husband's attitude to women) and would support the picture of a marriage that is not ideal. His highly-developed sexual fantasy may even suggest an erotic failure – so that Desdemona's use of the word "impotent" may hit a target more accurately than was intended.

17   Happiness to their Sheets

When Othello and Desdemona quit the Council Chamber in Act I his words to her are:

> Come, Desdemona, I have but an hour
> Of love, of worldly matters and direction
> To spend with thee. We must obey the time.

> (Act I, scene 3, 295-7)

If we take this last sentence to mean they are obliged to do what is expedient and politically required of them, then the "hour of love", especially as it is also filled with making practical arrangements, cannot, in fairness, include the consummation of the marriage. His words on arrival in Cyprus are so impassioned as to include sexual expectation. The honeymoon is still to be celebrated. Cassio talks of the prospect of Othello making "love's quick pants", in no way being prurient but rather seeing the event in terms of benediction. In Act II scene 2, we are told by the herald that it is the celebration of Othello's nuptial and the idea of benediction is reinforced. It is not long before Othello takes Desdemona by the hand with the words:

> The purchase made, the fruits are to ensue:
> That profit's yet to come 'tween me and you.

> (Act II, scene 3, 9-10)

In other words they are to enjoy the proper satisfaction of their first sexual union. This sentiment is distorted, once they have left the scene, into Iago's "He hath not yet made wanton the night with her; and she is sport for Jove". (It goes without saying that Jove was a highly promiscuous god). Iago goes as far as to imply that women's appetites are dangerously ungovernable.

Then of course all hell breaks loose with the drunken brawl, the ringing of the "dreadful bell" and the disturbance from their bed of the honeymooners. This is the enactment of the Chaos Othello fears as the alternative to loving.

70

Could we call this is a case of coitus interruptus? Evidence for this view may be adduced from the violence of the Moor's reactions:

> Why, how now, ho! From whence ariseth this?
> Are we turned Turks and to ourselves do that
> Which heaven hath forbid the Ottomites?
> For Christian shame, put by this barbarous brawl.
> He that stirs next to carve for his own rage
> Holds his soul light: he dies upon his motion.

(Act II, scene 3, 163-8)

Iago, disingenuously feigning reluctance, spills the beans, grassing on Cassio. The Moor, with what is meant to sound like the decisiveness of a General (though he is at the time a Governor), dismisses his lieutenant with peremptoriness of:

> Cassio, I love thee,
> But nevermore be officer of mine.

(Act II, scene 3, 242-3)

Notice the ambivalence ("love thee ... but") as well as the irony we may attach to the word "nevermore". It is at this moment that Desdemona surprisingly makes an appearance and provokes the further reaction:

> Look, if my gentle love be not raised up.
> I'll make thee an example.

(Act II, scene 3, 244-5)

(He will soon think in terms of making an example of Desdemona ... "else she'll betray more men.")

Either way (if they have indeed consummated their marriage or if the rite is still to ensue) Othello's rage may be said to spring from sexual thwarting. If it is the latter, then the lovers can hardly go back to it in a satisfactory frame of mind.

The argument that the marriage may never in fact achieve consummation can be reinforced by the notion of double-time in the play. Our experience in the theatre is one, not so much of chronological time, but of duration. The willing suspension of disbelief we experience serves to give the impression of continuous action. As there was no 'time' for an affair between Cassio and Desdemona, so there is now no psychological pause between this brawl and the poisoning of Othello's mind. It is quite possible to imagine consummation never occurring.

If we are right, then the play's terrifying logic ends in a symbolic consummation. Even if we believe an actual one has somehow, against all the odds, taken place, there still remains the possibility of seeing – either way – the play ending in this symbolic sexual union. Desdemona has ordered wedding sheets to be put on the bed and in the moment of his own death, according to the stage direction, Othello 'falls over her' on the bed with the words:

> I kissed thee, ere I killed thee: No way but this,
> Killing myself, to die upon a kiss.

> (Act V, scene 2, 354 - 5)

The original audience would have felt the force of the word "die" as containing sexual meaning: it meant to experience orgasm; sex was known as a 'little death.' So his death is, to say the least of it, a symbolic act of sex – and if it represents the proper satisfaction of a marriage-consummation the play takes on an unbearable poignancy.

With Desdemona's death, it had also reached a climax: the climax of all those meanings attaching themselves to the humour blood. Othello, first thinking of poisoning her, is persuaded to suffocate his wife, depriving her of the air, the element out of which the humour arises. Othello had welcomed the suggestion as poetic justice: "Good, good! The justice of it pleases; very good!"

18   It is the Cause

We have said that the play makes no distinction between sin and crime. Earthly justice is, ideally, the fulfilling of God's ordinance. We have to say 'ideally' because human justice works in the fallen world, in which angels and devils constantly battle for the possession of souls. It is therefore fallible. Human beings are always open to temptation and punishment is not always commensurate with the crime. One of the things tragedy makes us confront is that the good and the innocent have to pay a price too. And this is the point at which we have to fall back on Othello's "... but yet the pity of it, Iago. O, Iago, the pity of it".

Justice belongs to and requires authority. Whatever form this authority takes, be it King, Duke, Governor, these are conventionally figured as God's representatives on earth. In Venice the Duke represents justice. And yet he does not punish Othello for stealing away Brabantio's daughter, despite the fact that he tells the aggrieved father:

> Who'er he be that in this foul proceeding
> Hath thus beguiled your daughter of herself
> And you of her, the bloody book of law
> You shall yourself read in the bitter letter
> After your own sense, yea, though our proper son
> Stood in your action.

(Act I, scene 3, 65-70)

There is of course expediency as well as justice and the Duke is swayed both by Othello's eloquence and by the fact that he is at this particular moment politically and militarily irreplaceable. Desdemona's evidence is sought and one response to this scene that we cannot dismiss is Brabantio's:

> God bu'y. I have done.
> Please it your grace, on to the state affairs.
> I had rather to adopt a child than get it.
> Come hither, Moor:

I here do give thee that with all my heart
Which, but thou hast already, with all my heart
I would keep from thee.

(Act I, scene 3, 187-193)

The Duke ends the matter with aphoristic couplets which merely suggest a make-the-best-of-it philosophy and, though emotionally we too have been swayed by the honest forcefulness of the speeches we have heard, we still have in front of us on stage a broken-hearted father unlikely to be consoled by the Duke's words. Othello and Desdemona are *excused*: the fact that they have actually done wrong is almost forgotten. I say almost because something of it lingers in the back of our minds as too do his words "She has deceived her father and may thee" linger in the mind of Iago.

Othello is a top-notch military man and the justice he is used to is governed by the rules and conditions of war. It is usually peremptory, an eradicator of uncertainty. His decisiveness is a product of his training and experience as a soldier. "To be in doubt is once to be resolved." We have noticed how the storm neutralises his claim on victory and how his military experience, once brought into civil and private arenas, does not serve him well.

The death of Desdemona is seen as a summary execution. Desperately torn, he tries to persuade himself that he is, as Governor of Cyprus, enacting justice:

It is the cause, it is the cause, my soul:
Let me not name it to you, you chaste stars!
It is the cause.

(Act V, scene 2, 1-3)

The reference to the chaste stars (they might shudder at hearing the word 'adultery') tells us that he is thinking in terms of God's justice too. It is God's will, something absolute. Not knowing it, he is ironically subject to *hubris*. And yet he is tempted by other thoughts:

> O balmy breath, that dost almost persuade
> Justice to break her sword!

> (Act V, scene 2, 16-17)

The Christian in him is strong in this scene. Initially he gives her proper time to confess, to say her prayers and, therefore, throw herself on God's mercy. She already has her husband's compassion:

> I would not kill thy unprepared spirit;
> No – heaven forfend – I would not kill thy soul.

> (Act V, scene 2, 31-2)

What is being killed, then, is the corruptible body.

It has been said "the greatness of Iago lies in the fact that we never lose sympathy with Othello". Likewise, we might say that the tragedy of the noble Moor lies in the fact that he never stops loving his wife and that, when the plot against him is revealed, he has the courage to pass sentence and exact execution on himself.

All mortals, of course, have judgement – in the sense of reason. Remember it is Iago's intention to put Othello in to "a jealousy so strong that judgement cannot cure"; that he talks of Desdemona's "will recoiling to her better judgement".

It is a production decision as to whether we see Othello kill Desdemona, as it were, chastely enacting the decrees of justice or whether he kills her in a moment of passionate revenge. I am reminded of D.H. Lawrence's comment "Never hit a child except in anger" – the implication being that it is in this respect a *human* act. At the point of killing her he says of Cassio:

> Had all his hairs been lives, my great revenge
> Had stomach for them all.

> (Act V, scene 2, 76-6)

He goes on to denounce her as a strumpet, refusing her the chance to say one last prayer. This may be said to be tempered by the clemency implied in:

> Not dead? Not yet quite dead?
> I, that am cruel, am yet merciful:
> I would not have thee linger in thy pain.

(Act V, scene 2, 87-9)

But there again "Vengeance is mine, says the Lord". Has Othello damned himself by passionately murdering Desdemona or does he think he has justly executed her?

Poetic justice, too, is a necessary element in our experience. It is emotionally and aesthetically satisfying and contrived by writers to suggest to us that we live in – or at least their work inhabits – a moral universe, in which the guilty get their comeuppance. But it is only part of it. Tragedy exposes us to loss and waste too.

It is this sense of the loss of something good and noble that lies at the heart of tragedy and was part of what Aristotle was trying to describe with the word *catharsis* – his notion that the emotions of pity and terror are vicariously aroused in us and then purged away. But tragedy is about many things: it is about perception, identity ("I am what I am", "Men should be what they seem") and about what we value in human beings. It is a truism that we tend to value things once they are lost or their loss is threatened. But that is what tragedy shows us. It is about the dynamics of good and evil and, because of this, requires a divinity to preside over it and reassure us of an absolute justice.

We are left at the end with an impression that, after dreadful events and upheavals, order is somehow restorable – though those left behind to re-establish and represent order (and Shakespeare always hurries them off-stage) are pallid by comparison and rarely inspire confidence. That is why perhaps many productions end with survivors left with the job of picking up the pieces (for example Malcolm and MacDuff in *Macbeth)* giving each other meaningful looks, as if to say nothing has been settled after all.. The overwhelming feeling at the end of *Othello* is of uncompensatable loss, not just of the protagonist but also of those innocents caught up in the dreadful events witnessed. It is as if something irreplaceable has been taken away. Whether we are uplifted by this or thrown into a state of extreme perplexity depends very much upon the production.

19   One not Easily Jealous

If we believe that the play is simply about jealousy and that jealousy is, simplistically, the tragic flaw in Othello's character, we are likely to be unprepared for his claim at the end that he is "one not easily jealous".

Our account of him has been of the military man "declined into the vale of years", contemplating retirement and settling down (after becoming Venice's hero) where the good things of life are to be found; a man, if we are to believe John Leo's account of Moors, constitutionally hot-blooded ("wonderfully addicted to wrath"); a soldier all his life, single-minded in the pursuit of honour, knowing little of the ways of sophisticated Venice and, especially, its young women; whose experience and training expect decisiveness of him; who has fallen in love; whose sense of his own identity now rather extremely depends on it; who sadly underestimates the power of the blood (in its meaning of sexual passion). All of these things are known – either consciously or intuitively – by Iago determined on the Moor's destruction.

What we have to beware of is thinking that he deserves his fate (the loss of his wife and his own life) – i.e. that poetic justice enables us to say that he got no more than he deserved because he brought it all upon himself. This is not what tragedy is about.

Othello commits suicide. Is it a despairing act?:

> But every puny whipster gets my sword.
> But why should honour outlive honesty?
> Let it all go.

(Act V, scene 2, 242-4)

Indeed, why should honour outlive honesty? At this point in the play it is a good question. Is suicide an act of valour, the soldier's honourable exit? Is it an act of atonement, suggested by the reference to the "med'cinable gum" (myrrh)? A selfless act, committed in the spirit of cool justice (he is still the Governor) that he wished for in the 'execution' of his wife? Is it his last act of duty to the state? The whole of his final speech is concerned with the need for the state to understand he has been loyal to it. In one sense it is a political statement. It is also an assertion of the need all heroes feel for a true memorial.

Some critics would have us believe that the speech is simply further evidence of Othello's proclivity for self-dramatisation. T.S. Eliot sees the speech as the Moor "*cheering himself up*" (Eliot's italics) and "as endeavouring to escape reality ... Othello succeeds in turning himself into a pathetic figure, by adopting an *aesthetic* rather than a moral one, dramatizing himself against his environment. He takes in the spectator, but the human motive is primarily to take himself in."

Well, self-dramatisation is certainly part of the man's make-up. However, unlike Iago, who is a deliberate dissembler, he is perhaps not wholly aware of it – that is until the end. This is Aristotle's *anagnorisis*, the point to which tragedy ineluctably leads. "It is, after all," in the words of Clifford Leach "the last moment of consciousness ... the realisation of the unthinkable ... the point of no return." It is, in Aristotle's view, a change from ignorance to knowledge.

If we take Eliot's line the play becomes a melodrama and this is not most audience's experience of it. If we agree with him, we do not experience "the pity of it ... O the pity of it" and we would therefore need to subscribe to Iago's gleeful cynicism of "Thus credulous fools are caught".

I do not think it too far-fetched to suggest that if self-dramatisation is part of the man's identity – and always has been – then he now *knows* it and is actually being true to himself in this final act of self-dramatisation – just as vulnerably human as he has always been, still self-assertive in his desire for absolute certainty:

> Set you down this:
> And say, besides,that in Aleppo once
> Where a malignant and turbaned Turk
> Beat a Venetian and traduced the state,
> I took by th' throat the circumcisèd dog
> And smote him thus.

> (Act V, scene 2, 347-52)

If men should be what they seem, here is a man acting in character, asserting his noble identity with the need to do so still active and part of it. In a sense, what Othello is doing is executing the Iago under his own skin.

It is not an empty heroic flourish. It is done with the decisiveness and dignity that mark him out as a leader of men. The man has, as it were, looked into the mirror and seen himself for the first time as he really is. The measured cadences of the speech, the reticence are things we have learnt to admire. Something has been recovered (can one say redeemed?) but recovered too late. And this too-lateness is a crucial feature in tragedy. Gratiano underlines this, when Othello has stabbed himself, declaring "All that's spoke is marred!", as does Cassio with the words "For he was great of heart".

The direct simplicity of these statements are intended to carry a full weight. To question the truth of them is to collude with Iago.

What of the act of suicide? The orthodox Christian might be expected to think that the Moor has damned himself. Suicides went straight to hell. Othello, recovering his Christian poise at the end, knows this too. Gazing on the corpse of his wife he says:

> When we shall meet at compt
> This look of thine will hurl my soul from heaven
> And fiends will snatch at it. Cold, cold, my girl,
> Even like thy chastity.
> O cursèd, cursèd slave! Whip me, ye devils,
> From the possession of this heavenly sight!
> Blow me about in winds! Roast me in sulphur!
> Wash me in steep-down gulfs of liquid fire!

(Act V, scene 2, 271-8)

If we interpret this too as empty rhetoric then Iago and his view of the world are right: Othello was a gullible and stupid man who deserved what he got. There is no tragedy. Why should honour outlive dishonesty? The base Indian who "threw away a pearl richer than all his tribe" was a fool.

But Othello's judgement on himself isn't and cannot be the final one. In any case – in the above lines – he sees himself as going up to heaven on the Day of Judgement and being expelled from it. His own judgement on himself is not necessarily God's – nor indeed does it have to be the audience's. He himself imagines it as

Desdemona's (her now-proven chastity – virginity? – hurling his soul out of heaven); and it is an index of his love for and his grief at losing her.

Suicide – the Roman way of Cassius and Brutus – was for a soldier an honourable act. It is in this final act that Othello submits himself to judgement:

> Speak of me as I am: nothing extenuate,
> Nor set down aught in malice.

(Act V, scene 2, 338-9)

The idea of his being damned and lodged in hell is something we find ourselves needing to resist.

We would not feel the same about Iago.

Eliot's question from his *Choruses on the Rock*, "After such knowledge, what forgiveness?" is a real one. The tragedy of the Indian lies as much in his knowledge of loss – a pearl richer than all his tribe – as in the throwing away. He was someone:

> that loved not wisely, but too well;
> Of one not easily jealous but, being wrought,
> Perplexed in the extreme.

(Act V, scene 2, 340-2)

It is not primarily jealousy that undoes Othello (as it is with Leontes in *The Winter's Tale*); it is more complex than that. It is truer to say that it is jealousy that undoes Iago. It is more a matter of Othello's need for certainty and his innocence of the ways of the world outside the battlefield having been exploited by a malicious malcontent.

"For he was great of heart" is his epitaph.

The forgiveness of Othello – the play is, as it were, a set of extenuating circumstances to present at court on behalf of the accused – is outside our judgement. The world of the play implies that forgiveness of that order is God's. If God cannot forgive a man deemed to be great of heart, what hope is there for anyone else?

It may be said that tragic heroes have their roots in the rites of sacrifice, that they are sacrificial victims offered up as oblations.

They represent, with their failings included, a human best and are offered up on our behalf to make the gods more amenable. Christ may be seen as a tragic archetype, dying to redeem the world and give it hope.

20 Perdition Catch my Soul

Othello is an infernal play, constantly mindful of devils and perdition. When the overwhelming of the Turkish fleet in the storm is described as "mere perdition" ("mere" meaning absolute) the surface meaning is that of ruin and loss; but it also implies that, because the Turks are infidels (unbelievers), they have been properly consigned to Hell in an act of God ("all-judging Jove"). Hell, its inhabitants – both the damned and devils – are not, in this play, the stuff of fable. They are, as suggested earlier, an integral part of Elizabethan/Jacobean reality. Devils, like angels, come to earth and move about on it soliciting souls. If Hamlet can think that the ghost of his father may be a devil come to tempt him to perdition and if Marlowe, following the long tradition of bringing devils on stage, can thrill and/or amuse his audience by introducing Mephistopheles, then it is not at all farfetched for some of Shakespeare's audience to imagine Iago to be, in actuality, a devil. Othello thinks so – maybe wistfully – when, at the end, he says:

> I look down towards his feet; but that's a fable.
> If that thou be'st a devil, I cannot kill thee.

> (Act V, scene 2, 283-4)

He is referring to the fact that devils are said to have cloven hooves. But, as if in ironic confirmation, Iago, having been stabbed, sneers "I bleed, sir, but not killed". Othello's reply contains a profound irony:

> I am not sorry neither; I'd have thee live,
> For in my sense 'tis happiness to die.

> (Act V, scene 2, 286-7)

This from the man who had said on arrival in Cyprus "If it were now to die,/ 'Twere now to be most happy."

Othello, unwilling to give the idea up, is left with the term "demi-devil". Iago's fate is handed over to Cassio, the new Governor of

Cyprus:

> To you, Lord Governor,
> Remains the censure of this hellish villain:

(Act V, scene 2, 363-4)

At the beginning of the play, Iago tells Roderigo to plague Brabantio with flies (one name for the Devil or at least Beelzebub, is Lord of the Flies); he shouts that Brabantio will have "the devil make a grandsire of you". There are few things in the play that are not at one time or other labelled "devil". Othello is a devil in his blackness.

Iago's references to things hellish have made it certain that we at least think of him as being in league with the Devil. Of his machinations he says:

> Hell and night
> Must bring this monstrous birth to the world's light.

(Act I, scene 3, 397-8)

Women, to him, are "devils being offended"; he calls Cassio a "devilish knave"; during the Cyprus brawl he invokes "Diablo, ho!"; drunkenness and wrath are devils, as are sweating palms; in Act II, scene 3 he blasphemously invokes "Divinity of hell!" and tells us:

> When devils will the blackest sins put on,
> They do suggest at first with heavenly shows
> As I do now.

(Act II, scene 3, 341-3)

He tells Othello that people who dote yet doubt count "damnèd minutes"; cuckoldry is a forked plague (the devil wears horns); to lose the handkerchief:

> were such perdition
> As nothing else could match.

(Act III, scene 4, 67-8)

Iago describes Othello's valour on the battlefield as the action of a devil; Cassio tells Bianca to "throw your vile guesses in the devil's teeth"; the imagined affair is spoken of as:

> Naked in bed, Iago, and not mean harm?
> It is hypocrisy against the devil.
> They that mean virtuously and yet do so,
> The devil their virtue tempts, and they tempt heaven

(Act IV, scene 1, 5-8)

and:

> O, 'tis the spite of hell, the fiend's arch-mock,
> To lip a wanton in a secure couch,
> And to suppose her chaste!

(Act IV, scene 1, 70-2)

When Othello strikes Desdemona he calls her, with one of the play's supremest ironies, "Devil!" and when he questions her honesty in the bedroom he demands:

> Come, swear it; damn thyself;
> Lest being like one of heaven, the devils themselves
> Should fear to seize thee. Therefore be double-damned:
> Swear thou art honest.

(Act IV, scene 2, 34-7)

In his eyes, she is "false as hell"; he describes himself as looking "grim as hell"; Desdemona's attendant, Emilia, is said to be keeper of the "gate of hell" and she tells the Moor that her mistress is "more angel she,/ And you the blacker devil" and her husband that he has "told a lie, an odious damnèd lie":

> Let heaven, and men, and devils, let them all,
> All, all cry shame against me, yet I'll speak.

(Act V, scene 2, 219-20)

Iago, at the end, is recognised as a "Spartan dog", a "viper", a "hellish villain", even mistaken for the Fiend himself.

It goes without saying that opposites are always implied, always palpably present: heaven, angels, the saying of prayers, the chastity of stars, the constancy of true love. But in this play, just as the storm overwhelms the Turks, so we are involved in an emotional havoc and suffering, out of which, despite it all, is meant to emerge, however tenuously, some kind of hope.

21   Spartan Dog

Among the many dramatic strategies active in the play are those of seeing/not seeing (or not being seen) and hearing/not hearing (or speaking/not speaking). In the final scene we are asked to "look upon the tragic loading of this bed" as the culmination of all the seeing/ not seeing the play has been weaving together: Iago hiding his identity in the opening scene; later telling Othello "You were best go in"; Desdemona seeing her husband's "visage in his mind"; the Turkish fleet sailing towards Rhodes seen as "a pageant/ To keep us in false gaze"; the "ocular proof" of the handkerchief and so on. The play depends upon people not seeing things or seeing them through the distorting mirror of a corrupted and corrupting imagination.

There are many instances in which saying/not saying have dramatic impact: Cassio in Act II, scene 3 telling Othello "I pray you pardon me; I cannot speak"; Iago's feigned reluctance to speak to the Moor and finally dragging him down to the level of his own vile way of speaking; Emilia's "Let heaven, and men, and devils, let them all,/ All, all cry shame against me, yet I'll speak" and later her dying words "So come my soul to bliss, as I speak true;/ So speaking as I think, I die, I die." (We have already mentioned that dying words are conventionally intended to be taken as being true).

In the final scene, as a foil to Othello's noble and heart-breaking speeches, we have Iago's dumb insolence. When asked to explain his actions (do we imagine he *could* explain them?) he sneeringly replies:

> Demand me nothing; what you know, you know,
> From this time forth I never will speak word.

(Act V, scene 2, 300-1)

It is a superb moment: the words are spoken in absolute hate and with defiance. They suggest that, though he hasn't got away with it, he retains pride in his handiwork, in what he has achieved. The silence that follows these words is something else we take out of the theatre with us.

22   Dark Secret Love

Eldred Jones tells us that Othello:

> is taken (by some of the characters) as the manifestation of a
> type – the barbarous Moor, bond-slave, pagan – and he turns
> out to be noble Christian, if somewhat naïve. We thus have a
> double antithesis: Iago is both soldier and villain, Othello is
> both Moor and noble hero.

The symmetry of this equation suggests another way of looking
at the relationship between Othello and Iago, one already implied in
the Blake poem quoted earlier: that is to see it as symbiotic. The
startling word in Blake's *Sick Rose* is "love" ("and his dark secret
love") and not the 'hate' we might expect in a process of destruction.
It also recalls the perfect symmetry of Blake's *The Clod & the Pebble*:

> Love seeketh not Itself to please,
> Nor for itself hath any care;
> But for another gives its ease,
> And builds a Heaven in Hells despair.

> So sang a little Clod of Clay,
> Trodden with the cattles feet:
> But a Pebble of the brook,
> Warbled out these metres meet.

> Love seeketh only Self to please,
> To bind another to its delight;
> Joys in anothers loss of ease,
> And builds a Hell in Heaven's despite.

Can it be said that both these men are soul-mates; that they 'need'
each other and that both of them carry within them a death-wish
which the other makes real? This would require us to consider Iago
as hero-worshipping the Moor and unforgivingly resenting his
slighting of him and then 'seducing' him into a fearful amity. In other
words, each nurtures in the other the seeds of self-destruction already
implanted in them. Does it mean that Blake's rose and worm, in the

natural order of things, need each other, rely upon each other for the business of life itself? The relationship between "the two contrary states of the human soul" that Blake expresses in his *Songs of Innocence and Experience* is a dynamic one. Which of the two – heaven or hell – is winning?

Conclusion – A Word or Two Before you Go

In *Othello* Shakespeare has shown us an extravagant and wheeling stranger, a valiant Moor, turned Christian, hoping to settle down and live the rest of his life in civilised Venice with a woman with whom he has eloped, but who is tragically denied his wish. The full title of the play – *Othello the Moor of Venice* – is an ironic one: Othello is not allowed to put down roots in Venice: he is made governor of Cyprus and dies there.

Shakespeare wants us to see the man beneath the skin and understand that nobility is not a matter of colour or race. Flying in the face of all the negative associations of blackness, he challengingly gives us a black man for hero and a white man for villain. Honour and honesty are key issues, as are the dynamic weaving together of tensions between opposites that inform the action.

It has been called the most concentrated of the four major tragedies – though *Macbeth* can also lay claims to this. It is certainly driven by a terrifying 'logic' to an inescapable climax. Iago's machinations – his plot to possess the heart and mind of the Moor – come to focus in the long 'seduction' scene (Act III, scene 3) in which Othello gives himself up to Iago ("Now art thou my Lieutenant"). I say 'seduction' deliberately since one of the play's most obvious ingredients is sexual tension – which Iago spins out of himself like a spider to catch his victims. After this scene, the play moves relentlessly to its murderous climax, which takes place before our eyes. We are spared nothing.

If *Hamlet* and *Lear* are about child/parent relationships, *Macbeth* and *Othello* may be said to be about marriage. But *Othello* is not, as some have suggested, a great love story (*Antony and Cleopatra* would be a better candidate): if it is about marriage it is about one only in embryo. Dover Wilson for example in his introduction to the Cambridge New Shakespeare edition of the play declares Othello to be "the greatest lover in Shakespeare", whose love for Desdemona "confirms his faith in the harmony and stability of the universe". I do not think it helpful to see the relationship between Othello and Desdemona as some sort of spiritual union, a union of noble souls. This is not to say that the play hasn't much to tell us about love and how difficult it is to get it right. It is a story about the beginnings of love, of dangerous infatuations with no time or opportunity to mature into the kind of love human beings constantly dream of as perfect. The marriage between Desdemona and Othello is a relationship based on hope rather than achievement and it is built on shaky foundations – as is Othello's Christianity, and he knows it. And Iago knows it too and uses the knowledge to bring about his downfall. Othello carries within him the seeds of his own destruction. Pushkin was right when he asserted "Othello was not jealous by nature, he was trustful". The truly jealous person in the play is Iago. And he is no genius but rather a vulgar, small-minded man – clever and crafty maybe but not the evil genius of Romantic critics.

There are inconsistencies in the play. For example, why didn't Brabantio see what was going on in the courtship? Is Roderigo's gullibility altogether credible? Why did Othello see that there was no time or space for adultery between Desdemona and Cassio to have taken place? Is the handkerchief not a rather too obvious plot device? These are things we might notice in reading but in performance the pace of the play and the audience's willing suspension of disbelief do not allow sufficient pause in which to ask these questions. This is sometimes called Double Time, a matter of pace rather than duration.

I have tried to see the play and its characters in Renaissance terms because I think these are not only helpful towards a possible interpretation but act as safeguards against possible misinterpretation. Of course it transcends these. As Ben Jonson declared, Shakespeare was for all time. There will always be suffering; sexual jealousy will continue to tear at people's emotions, however enlightened they suppose themselves to be; people will continue to let their hearts rule their heads and there will always be killjoys, destroyers of others' happiness. The world of the rose is also the world of the invisible worm. *Othello* is about human aspiration, the freedom and ability to choose and pursue good rather than evil. What tragedies like this seem to offer is the spectacle of an ostensibly good person tried and tested in the arena of truth and measured by what we might call the quality of their suffering. We rejoice in the nobility with which they confront their fate and sorrow in the loss of human potential. What is gained in tragedy is truth paid for with the very high price of death. The battle is between the good in our natures and the bad, between our strengths and weaknesses. It's as old as time. The tragic hero, I have suggested, may be related to the sacrificial victim, as offering to appease the gods in what the Chorus in *Oedipus Rex* calls "the encounters of man with more than man". As George Steiner says in *The Death of Tragedy*, "tragedy is that form of art which requires the intolerable burden of God's presence".

That is the optimist view and we need to believe in nobility to sustain it. There are those who would see things nihilistically: that in the tragic hero's choice of all or nothing nothing, is the outcome. All is for nothing. Human beings act out their lives without any ultimate purpose. But Shakespeare has not written Absurd dramas. As the *Princeton Encyclopedia of Poetry and Poetics* puts it "A negative or moralistc approach to tragedy undervalues the hero's strength and in effect short-circuits the tragic experience." Shakespeare's purpose may be said to be similar to that expressed in these lines from an anonymous play of 1599 entitled *A Warning for Fair Women*:

> I must have passions that must move the soul;
> Make the heart heavy and throb within the bosom,
> Extorting tears out of the strictest eyes –
> To rack a thought, and strain it from its form,
> Until I rap the senses from their course.
> This is my office.

Bibliography

A.C. Bradley, *Shakespearean Tragedy* (Macmillan, 1904)

Jonathan Bate, *The Genius of Shakespeare* (Picador, 1997)

Harold Bloom, *Shakespeare, the Invention of the Human* (Fourth Estate, 1999)

Lily B. Campbell, *Shakespeare's Tragic Heroes* (Cambridge, 1930)

Samuel Taylor Coleridge, *Shakespearean Criticism* (Dent, 1961)

T.S. Eliot, *Shakespeare and the Stoicism of Seneca, Selected Essays* (Faber, 1932)

William Empson, *The Structure of Complex Words* (Methuen, 1951)

David Gervais, *The Comic Muse* (PNR Vol. 29, No. 2 pp35-8, 2002)

Harley Granville-Barker, *Prefaces to Shakespeare Vol IV* (Batsford, 1946)

Robert Heilman, *The Magic Web* (University of Kentucky Press, 1952)

Anthony Holden, *William Shakespeare – his Life and his Work* (Abacus, 1999)

Eldred Jones, *Othello's Countrymen, the African in English Renaissance Drama* (Oxford, 1965)

The Wheel of Fire, G. Wilson Knight (Oxford, 1930)

Clifford Leach, *Tragedy* (The Critical Idiom Series Methuen, 1975)

F.R. Leavis, *The Common Pursuit* (Penguin, 1952)

Geoffrey Matthews, '*Othello and the Dignity of Man*' *Shakespeare in a Changing World, Essays,* ed. Arnold Kettle (Lawrence & Wishart, 1971)

Sir Walter Raleigh, *Shakespeare* (English Men of Letters, 1907)

E.M.W. Tillyard, *The Elizabethan World Picture* (Chatto & Windus, 1943)

John Wain, *The Living World of Shakespeare* (Penguin, 1964)

I have used *The New Penguin Shakespeare* throughout. The quotations from Marlowe are from *The Penguin English Library* edition of the plays and the Shakespeare sonnets are from Martin Seymour-Smith's edition of 2001. I have taken the liberty of adding an accent to "fixèd" in line 5 of No 116. and have retained the punctuation and layout of Blake's poems as they are found in *The Complete Poems* edited by Alicia Ostriker (Penguin, 1979). The translation of a passage from Giraldo Cinthio's *Hecatommithi* is that of J.E. Taylor and also found in the Signet edition of the play.

GREENWICH EXCHANGE BOOKS

Greenwich Exchange Student Guides are critical studies of major or contemporary serious writers in English and selected European languages. The series is for the student, the teacher and 'common readers' and is an ideal resource for libraries. The *Times Educational Supplement* (*TES*) praised these books, saying, "The style of these guides has a pressure of meaning behind it. Students should learn from that ... If art is about selection, perception and taste, then this is it."

(ISBN prefix 1-871551- applies)
The series includes:
W.H. Auden by Stephen Wade (-36-6)
Honoré de Balzac by Wendy Mercer (48-X)
William Blake by Peter Davies (-27-7)
The Brontës by Peter Davies (-24-2)
Robert Browning by John Lucas (-59-5)
Samuel Taylor Coleridge by Andrew Keanie (-64-1)
Joseph Conrad by Martin Seymour-Smith (-18-8)
William Cowper by Michael Thorn (-25-0)
Charles Dickens by Robert Giddings (-26-9)
John Donne by Sean Haldane (-23-4)
Thomas Hardy by Sean Haldane (-35-1)
Seamus Heaney by Warren Hope (-37-4)
Philip Larkin by Warren Hope (-35-8)
Laughter in the Dark – The Plays of Joe Orton by Arthur Burke (56-0)
Philip Roth by Paul McDonald (72-2)
Shakespeare's Non-Dramatic Poetry by Martin Seymour-Smith (22-6)
Shakespeare's Sonnets by Martin Seymour Smith (38-2)
Tobias Smollett by Robert Giddings (-21-8)
Alfred Lord Tennyson by Michael Thorn (-20-X)
William Wordsworth by Andrew Keanie (57-9)

OTHER GREENWICH EXCHANGE BOOKS
Paperback unless otherwise stated.

Shakespeare's Sonnets
Martin Seymour-Smith
Martin Seymour-Smith's outstanding achievement lies in the field of literary biography and criticism. In 1963 he produced his comprehensive edition, in the old spelling, of *Shakespeare's Sonnets* (here revised and corrected by himself and Peter Davies in 1998). With its landmark introduction and

its brilliant critical commentary on each sonnet, it was praised by William Empson and John Dover Wilson. Stephen Spender said of him "I greatly admire Martin Seymour-Smith for the independence of his views and the great interest of his mind"; and both Robert Graves and Anthony Burgess described him as the leading critic of his time. His exegesis of the *Sonnets* remains unsurpassed.

2001 • 194 pages • ISBN 1-871551-38-2

English Language Skills

Vera Hughes

If you want to be sure, as a student, or in your business or personal life,) that your written English is correct, this book is for you. Vera Hughes' aim is to help you remember the basic rules of spelling, grammar and punctuation. 'Noun', 'verb', 'subject', 'object' and 'adjective' are the only technical terms used. The book teaches the clear, accurate English required by the business and office world. It coaches acceptable current usage and makes the rules easier to remember.

Vera Hughes was a civil servant and is a trainer and author of training manuals.

2002 • 142 pages • ISBN 1-871551-60-9

LITERARY CRITICISM

The Author, the Book and the Reader

Robert Giddings

This collection of essays analyses the effects of changing technology and the attendant commercial pressures on literary styles and subject matter. Authors covered include Charles Dickens, Tobias George Smollett, Mark Twain, Dr Johnson and John le Carré.

1991 • 220 pages • illustrated • ISBN 1-871551-01-3

Liar! Liar!: Jack Kerouac – Novelist

R.J. Ellis

The fullest study of Jack Kerouac's fiction to date. It is the first book to devote an individual chapter to every one of his novels. *On the Road, Visions of Cody* and *The Subterraneans* are reread in-depth, in a new and exciting way. *Visions of Gerard* and *Doctor Sax* are also strikingly reinterpreted, as are other daringly innovative writings, like 'The Railroad Earth' and his "try at a spontaneous *Finnegan's Wake*" – *Old Angel Midnight*. Neglected writings, such as *Tristessa* and *Big Sur*, are also analysed, alongside better-known novels such as *Dharma Bums* and *Desolation Angels*.

R.J. Ellis is Senior Lecturer in English at Nottingham Trent University.
1999 • 295 pages • ISBN 1-871551-53-6

BIOGRAPHY

The Good That We Do
John Lucas
John Lucas' book blends fiction, biography and social history in order to tell the story of his grandfather, Horace Kelly. Headteacher of a succession of elementary schools in impoverished areas of London, 'Hod' Kelly was also a keen cricketer, a devotee of the music hall, and included among his friends the great Trade Union leader, Ernest Bevin. In telling the story of his life, Lucas has provided a fascinating range of insights into the lives of ordinary Londoners from the First World War until the outbreak of the Second World War. Threaded throughout is an account of such people's hunger for education, and of the different ways government, church and educational officialdom ministered to that hunger. *The Good That We Do* is both a study of one man and of a period when England changed, drastically and forever.
John Lucas is Professor of English at Nottingham Trent University and is a poet and critic.
2001 • 214 pages • ISBN 1-871551-54-4

In Pursuit of Lewis Carroll
Raphael Shaberman
Sherlock Holmes and the author uncover new evidence in their investigations into the mysterious life and writing of Lewis Carroll. They examine published works by Carroll that have been overlooked by previous commentators. A newly discovered poem, almost certainly by Carroll, is published here.
Amongst many aspects of Carroll's highly complex personality, this book explores his relationship with his parents, numerous child friends, and the formidable Mrs Liddell, mother of the immortal Alice. Raphael Shaberman was a founder member of the Lewis Carroll Society and a teacher of autistic children.
1994 • 118 pages • illustrated • ISBN 1-871551-13-7

Musical Offering
Yolanthe Leigh
In a series of vivid sketches, anecdotes and reflections, Yolanthe Leigh tells the story of her growing up in the Poland of the 30s and the Second World War. These are poignant episodes of a child's first encounters with both the enchantments and the cruelties of the world; and from a later time, stark

memories of the brutality of the Nazi invasion, and the hardships of student life in Warsaw under the Occupation. But most of all this is a record of inward development; passages of remarkable intensity and simplicity describe the girl's response to religion, to music, and to her discovery of philosophy.

Yolanthe Leigh was formerly a Lecturer in Philosophy at Reading University.

2000 • 57 pages • ISBN: 1-871551-46-3

Norman Cameron

Warren Hope

Norman Cameron's poetry was admired by W.H. Auden, celebrated by Dylan Thomas and valued by Robert Graves. He was described by Martin Seymour-Smith as, "one of ... the most rewarding and pure poets of his generation ..." and is at last given a full length biography. This eminently sociable man, who had periods of darkness and despair, wrote little poetry by comparison with others of his time, but always of a consistently high quality – imaginative and profound.

2000 • 221 pages • illustrated • ISBN 1-871551-05-6

POETRY

Adam's Thoughts in Winter

Warren Hope

Warren Hope's poems have appeared from time to time in a number of literary periodicals, pamphlets and anthologies on both sides of the Atlantic. They appeal to lovers of poetry everywhere. His poems are brief, clear, frequently lyrical, characterised by wit, but often distinguished by tenderness. The poems gathered in this first book-length collection counter the brutalising ethos of contemporary life, speaking of and for the virtues of modesty, honesty and gentleness in an individual, memorable way.

2000 • 47 pages • ISBN 1-871551-40-4

Baudelaire: Les Fleurs du Mal

Translated by F.W. Leakey

Selected poems from *Les Fleurs du Mal* are translated with parallel French texts and are designed to be read with pleasure by readers who have no French as well as those who are practised in the French language.

F.W. Leakey was Professor of French in the University of London. As a scholar, critic and teacher he specialised in the work of Baudelaire for 50 years and published a number of books on the poet.

2001 • 153 pages • ISBN 1-871551-10-2

Lines from the Stone Age
Sean Haldane
Reviewing Sean Haldane's 1992 volume *Desire in Belfast*, Robert Nye wrote in *The Times* that "Haldane can be sure of his place among the English poets." This place is not yet a conspicuous one, mainly because his early volumes appeared in Canada and because he has earned his living by other means than literature. Despite this, his poems have always had their circle of readers. The 60 previously unpublished poems of *Lines from the Stone Age* – "lines of longing, terror, pride, lust and pain" – may widen this circle.
2000 • 53 pages • ISBN 1-871551-39-0

Wilderness
Martin Seymour-Smith
This is Martin Seymour-Smith's first publication of his poetry for more than 20 years. This collection of 36 poems is a fearless account of an inner life of love, frustration, guilt, laughter and the celebration of others. He is best known to the general public as the author of the controversial and bestselling *Hardy* (1994).
1994 • 52 pages • ISBN 1-871551-08-0